My Country wept

'Any reader of this book having an open mind and heart will be inspired by the wonderful providential love of God revealed in the life and experiences of Theo. Furthermore, Theo's faith and courage is an outstanding example and challenge for all readers, be they Christians or not.'

Canon Stanley Dakin

'Jess Komanapalli has written an important work that should be read by everyone. When love overcomes the violence and hate of war, a story of redemption, salvation and hope remains.

'This story is an extraordinary journey of survival through faith, challenges overcome and the small, unexpected moments of grace that allow us to hold onto our faith in the midst of the horrors of war. Theo faced death at every turn as he navigated the civil war raging through his home. He survived to tell his tale. Through his telling, may you find the courage to see God's almighty presence in every trial you face.

'This book is the story of how one young man looked to God to save him, teach him, and had the courage and passion to save others. It is in this great hope – the understanding that we are all called to forgive and serve, have the patience to allow the process to unfold and the fortitude to endure it – that the Lord will shine his light to a weary world.

'I highly recommend the reading of *My Country Wept*.'

Scott Norling, International Consultant Asia Director,
Joyce Meyer Ministries

'Theo's story is deeply moving and powerful. He tells of some of the sorrows and sufferings of his beloved and beautiful nation, Burundi. His life's journey reveals both the amazing rescue and calling of God without avoiding the hard question of why he has stayed alive whilst others have tragically died. I was moved deeply by his honesty and by the mercy of God at work in him.

'This book will inspire and help all readers discover more of God in Jesus Christ. It will also help readers understand more of the history and shaping of the nation that is both beautiful and tragic Burundi.'

Paul Butler, Bishop of Durham

'A breathtaking sweep through the eyes of a man who has been saved by grace multiple times amid enduring and generational mess in East Africa. This book takes your breath away, it's written with such gritty reality and reflects ultimately on the Saviour whom Theo loves and follows. Inspirational, and everyone who seeks to understand how to engage across cultures in missional life and work needs to read this book.'

Andy Dipper, Principal & Chief Executive,
All Nations Christian College

'What a compelling story of survival, strength of character, "unexplainable" miracles, and the undeniable belief that God watches over us.

'It is a wonderful true story of how God can bring a life out of darkness, peace through forgiveness, restitution and hope from pain.

'It challenges each one of us to make a difference in our world today. Bless Burundi.'

Susan Botta, Senior Pastor, C3 Church Carlingford,
Sydney, Australia

'In telling his story so vividly, honestly and respectfully, Theodore has rendered a great service to the whole nation of

Burundi. It is my strong conviction that in listening together to personal stories of pain and suffering like his, a genuine mutual compassion can emerge and the road for forgiveness and reconciliation gets paved. I whole-heartedly recommend this book.'

Emmanuel Ndikumana, Founder and President of Partners Trust International, Regional Director for the Lausanne Movement for Francophone Africa and Board Chair for the Great Lakes Initiatives for Reconciliation

'Theo went through ordeal after ordeal which would make anyone give up their hope of survival, but he encountered victory after victory, and proof that God protects his own, no matter what kind of fiery circumstances they go through.'

Reverend Rachel Komanapalli, Co-Founder, Manna Group of Ministries, India

My Country Wept

One man's incredible story of faith, hope and forgiveness in the Burundian civil war

Jess Komanapalli

Authentic

Copyright © 2018 Jess Komanapalli

24 23 22 21 20 19 18   8 7 6 5 4 3 2

First published 2018 by Authentic Media Limited,
PO Box 6326, Bletchley, Milton Keynes, MK1 9GG.
authenticmedia.co.uk
Reprinted 2018

British Library Cataloguing in Publication Data
A catalogue record for this book is available from the British Library.
ISBN: 978-1-78078-464-9
978-1-78078-465-6 (e-book)

Scripture quotations taken from
The Holy Bible, New International Version Anglicised
© 1979, 1984, 2011 Biblica
Used by permission of Hodder & Stoughton Ltd, an Hachette UK company.
All rights reserved.
'NIV' is a registered trademark of Biblica
UK trademark number 1448790.

Some names in this book have been changed to protect the identity of individuals.

Cover design by Arnel Gregorio
arrowdesigns01@gmail.com

Printed in the UK by CPI Group (UK) Ltd., Croydon, CR0 4YY

Contents

Foreword ix

1 Secrets of the Past 1
2 The Promise 13
3 Godance's Help 25
4 A Difficult Decision 33
5 In the Forest 41
6 Together Again 53
7 Disease and Death 63
8 A Ray of Hope 73
9 Mtabila 80
10 Making Amends 90
11 Bushman 98
12 Papa 105
13 Escape 113
14 Caught! 123
15 Behind Bars 133
16 Case Closed 143
17 On to Nairobi 154
18 God's Provision 162
19 An Offer of a Lifetime 170

20	An Amazing Door	192
21	The Promise Fulfilled	204
	Epilogue	211
	Acknowledgments	217
	Further Information	219

Foreword

It's a strange thing to talk to someone who should really be long dead.

What you have in front of you is quite simply an extraordinary story. Time and again, it looked like Theo's life was about to end, only for God to provide a miraculous escape. Had he died – as many of his beloved countrymen did – we would never have heard of him; but he survived to tell the tale, and so now you and I get the chance to read it and be challenged and impacted by it.

I've known Theo for over a decade now and am proud to call him my friend. We spent a year studying together in England at All Nations Christian College, before both returning to our overlapping mission fields in Burundi. And having suffered so much as a refugee himself, Theo has exhibited relentless courage, passion and energy in helping other marginalised and dispossessed people find justice and restitution. I greatly admire this man of respect and integrity, and hope you will be deeply moved through reading his story.

War-time Burundi and the camps in Tanzania were dark places. Yet it's in the darkest places that the light shines brightest. God never abandoned Theo. His faith took many knocks,

Anger rose from the pit of my stomach, sweeping through every inch of me.

It was clear to me that my teacher had jumped at the chance to lash out at me again. Had I been just a single minute late, I was sure my fate would have been the same.

It wasn't the first time I felt I had been unfairly reprimanded. These harsh beatings happened every time a mistake was spotted in my schoolwork – every time I was caught not paying attention to the blackboard – every time I was seen talking to my classmates while the teacher explained a new exercise or rule.

I was just 11 years old and, to my mind, I had every right to be enraged at the beating my teacher had just given me – and at every other heavy beating that had preceded it.

Through my eyes, my teacher's actions were hateful acts of injustice and I felt sick to my core when I thought about the reason behind them. Less than half a year back, my father had revealed a secret of his that had taught me this reason and much more besides.

'Sit down now, Theo!' my teacher barked, interrupting my vivid recollections of that day. He turned to the blackboard to find his chalk.

But I knew I wouldn't be able to obey. I just couldn't bring myself to. Not after remembering the painful truths I was now aware of. I was too angry. Far too angry.

Before I could stop myself, my mouth had opened and I was spitting out an incensed accusation.

The words drew instant gasps of disbelief and the full attention of my fellow classmates.

'I know why you always beat me! It's because I'm a Hutu and you're a Tutsi! And you've been killing our people since 1972!'

My teacher spun around to face me. His alarmed expression met my raging stare. Starting to open his mouth, he quickly shut it again.

He was speechless. After all, how was he supposed to respond to such an outburst? No one would have ever dared to challenge him, let alone mention the things I had just mentioned.

But I had truly had enough. I refused to be subject to his cruel punishments any longer just because I had been born a Hutu, and he a Tutsi.

'Go outside!' my teacher demanded, regaining his voice. 'Get out of the classroom!'

This time I chose to obey, kicking up dust on the dirt floor as I bolted out through the door. Sticking close to the brick wall of our school building, I came to stand beside the paneless window frame which looked in on my class.

My whole body was shaking and my heart pounded in my chest – partly out of anger and partly from the adrenaline which had been churned up by my audacious act.

My classmates remained quiet and, peeking in, I could see my teacher had returned to the blackboard to write the day's lesson.

I showed him! I thought. *That evil Tutsi! I should have taken his cane and struck him back! Beating me so badly for being ten minutes late! I really showed him!*

I hated my teacher and wished I could inflict on him the same punishments he had tortured me with. But the reality was, my hatred for him and his vicious punishments wasn't the only frustration at the heart of my anger that day.

This was because, as a result of what my father had shared with me months earlier, I had been harbouring a mixture of pent-up emotions that had finally come to the surface when my teacher had dared to beat me cruelly again.

My Country Wept

The Tutsi men said nothing more, either. Some just smirked menacingly while others looked us up and down with distaste. Their eyes glistened with a hatred I had never seen before.

Suddenly, one of the group turned and nodded to the other men.

Then they started to close in around us.

Oh no! Please . . . no!

Several of the men braced their weapons in their hands, ready to strike.

No! Please, Lord!

'Stop! Stop!'

A loud cry coming from the side made us all turn our heads.

From the corner of my eye, I saw someone running in our direction.

It was a woman and she was headed straight towards us.

What's happening? I thought. *Who is she?*

Who could have predicted what began to unfold next?

3

Godance's Help

'Theo! *Theo!*' the woman's voice called.

Was that my name I was hearing?

The woman pushed past the men and put her arms around me.

'Stop!' she yelled. 'You have to stop! Don't harm them.'

I tried to comprehend what was happening and caught sight of her face.

It was one I recognised – the woman was my friend, Godance!

Godance and I had been in the same school together a few years previously. I had often helped her with difficult maths or science problems. We had lost touch after she had moved to a different school. More significant to our predicament, Godance was a Tutsi.

To my amazement, she addressed the gang of men directly.

'If you want to kill them, you better kill me first!' Godance said. 'These are my friends. They are good people!'

She is crazy! I thought. *Why is she doing this? They will kill her, too!*

But I was paralysed with fear. I couldn't even breathe, let alone open my mouth to say anything to stop Godance.

As her arms clung tightly around my neck, the men stared at Godance, still not saying anything.

I was certain they would murder her first right in front of us. Then we would all be next.

The stand-off seemed to last an eternity.

I watched the eyes of the men darting between us all. They were considering what to do next.

And then something unimaginable happened.

Slowly, with some grumbling and muttering, the men conferred. Then they began to disband around us.

All six of us blinked in disbelief.

They are listening to her! They are really listening!

It was apparent these Tutsis knew Godance and held her in great respect. We later found out this was because her brother was a high-ranking officer in the Army.

But at that moment, all we knew was that they were afraid to challenge Godance. They were walking away from us and letting us go free!

We had been certain we were about to be murdered. Yet our lives had been spared again.

How had we been so lucky? Was God really protecting us?

Shaking with relief, I clutched Godance's hand. I had not seen her in more than three years.

'What are you doing here?' I managed to ask, still breathless with terror. 'Why did you do that for us?'

'You're my friend, Theo,' she said. 'I couldn't let them hurt you. But let's not talk now; come this way.' She beckoned to us to follow her. 'My home is not too far away. It's not safe to linger here.'

Godance let us rest in her house for a while and gave us some food and water. We ate quickly, relieving our hunger while being eager to leave as soon as we could. We were afraid the men might return to find us.

For our safety, Godance insisted she escort us through her village until we had reached an area she felt the Tutsi mob would not pursue us through. I was overwhelmed by her act of kindness and bravery – she was still willing to put herself at risk to help us.

'We cannot thank you enough for what you did for us,' I told Godance as we said our goodbyes. 'There are no words I can find to express our gratitude.'

'You have no need to thank me,' Godance told us as she left us. 'My care is just for your safety. May God keep you all on your way.'

I hoped in my heart that we would see each other again, in happier and peaceful times.

More than the providence of Godance spotting us and saving our lives, what astounded me the most was what she had done for us. We hadn't been especially close to each other – just simple classmates – yet she had stood in front of the blood-hungry mob and been ready to sacrifice her life to save me and my friends. I had never seen another human display such qualities before. It was a show of courage and love which reminded me of stories about Jesus.

Because of this, meeting my old school friend had a profound and lasting impact on me.

God had not just spared our lives, but had used the least likely person – a Tutsi – to do this. That day, I felt challenged to alter my way of thinking. Before, my anger at our country's conflict had been directed towards Tutsis as a group. But God had used Godance to show me that not everyone was the same. Perhaps the blame lay largely with the politicians and people in power, I now reasoned. I could not blame all Tutsis. Yes, there were some bad Tutsis. But wasn't it true that there were some bad Hutus, too? Instead, the astounding love Godance had shown us gave me a strong conviction:

I cannot dislike and blame every Tutsi for this war. I must treat every Tutsi I meet as an individual.

It was a realisation that would form the basis of an important journey I had to make in the future – one of reconciliation with those I considered to be my enemies.

During our short time with Godance, our group had made a significant decision. This was to split up. Many of us were close to our family homes and Godance had assured us it would be safe to take a detour and travel to see them. As much as we needed to escape the country, we were still desperate to know what had become of our parents, siblings and other loved ones. We were all willing to take the risk of returning to our homes to find out.

'Let's hope we meet again in Tanzania,' I said, as I bid each boy farewell before they set off on their way. 'God has shown us he can save our lives. Go quickly and pray that he will protect us all.' We departed, wondering how many of us would make it across the border.

I felt a mixture of hope and fear as I undertook the five-hour walk to my father's house, which was in a village called Ruhinga. There was ample time to imagine the different scenarios that might greet me when I arrived. Perhaps I would be fortunate enough to find my parents and siblings safe and well at our home. It would be a comforting reunion and I could already picture my parents' joy and relief at seeing me again. Or perhaps I would find no one there at all. My family might have already fled elsewhere. Other possibilities were too distressing to dwell on.

As I arrived at my village, I was greeted by a smell that was horrific. I retched when my nose picked up the putrid scent of rotting flesh. My eyes were soon drawn to a harrowing sight – a number of dead bodies were lying in the fields and by the roadside. Passing a few and gaining a closer look at the corpses, my horror intensified. These were the dead bodies of friends and villagers I had grown up with. My neighbour Misigaro's beaten and bloated body lay by the side of the road. We had been in the same class throughout elementary school. Then I saw my neighbour Mariko's corpse exposed by the edge of a field. He was a kind man who used to keep cows. I turned my face away, not wanting to discover how he had been killed.

Both of these men had been Tutsis.

No! No! I cannot be seeing this! Are they really all dead?

It was the hardest thing to accept – seeing people I recognised, brutally murdered, with no respect for their life at all. I felt that my own life at that moment had little value, too. It could easily be extinguished without a care.

What upset me even further were the stick-thin dogs which surrounded most of the bodies. Their hunger was so great, they stood feasting on the corpses. I wished I could close my eyes to the sight. To me, this was an indication of how distressing times had become. Just as in biblical days, Burundians shared the belief that to die without burial, allowing animals to eat at your corpse, was the worst punishment that could befall anyone. But there was no one here to bury the dead. My home village had become a ghost town. Its empty streets indicated that many had fled, leaving their houses and belongings.

I saw that some homes had even been torched and lay in collapsed remains.

Just moments later, a few villagers who had remained came out to see me. 'Where are my parents and family?' I questioned them, anxiously. 'Are they at home? Has anyone been hurt?'

One neighbour told me: 'They must be alive. They left for Tanzania already.'

Thank you, Lord!

It was a huge relief that they had not been harmed. I had already started to fear the worst.

A small part of me was also disappointed to learn that my family had left and I wouldn't see them, but I knew it was much better news they had managed to escape.

The neighbour told me as much as he knew, including what else had happened in our village.

He related that straight after the President's assassination was reported, some of our Hutu villagers had set upon their Tutsi neighbours, torching their houses and killing them with machetes. This, despite the fact they had once been friends with the same neighbours. Now entire families had been wiped out. He listed the names of both the murderers and the murdered. I knew them all. I had gone to school with some of them. My heart was full of despair, trying to comprehend what the war had done to us.

'Then in retaliation for the killings,' he continued, 'the Army arrived and began to shoot into the village. This is when most of the people fled from here, including your family.'

I arrived at our family home to find it empty. The doors and windows were broken. Entering in, it was obvious someone had ransacked the place. My family's belongings were strewn all over the floor. I went into the different rooms, not knowing what I was looking for but perhaps hoping something might be salvaged of the place we had once called home. Walking into my mother and father's bedroom, I spotted a pair of my father's rolled-up socks on the floor. They weren't clean socks and I had no need for them but for some reason my eyes were drawn to them. I picked them up and was startled by what I found when I unrolled them. They were full of Burundian francs that my father had hidden – 5,000 in total, the equivalent of 12 US dollars at that time. I stuffed the notes into my pocket. I had fled my school without any money and it would certainly be useful.

I had been battling my hunger pains all day and my attention turned to finding some food. I decided to go outside to see if I could catch and kill one of my father's chickens. A few of them were still walking about in our compound. But then, glancing across the road, I caught sight of some other chickens roaming within my neighbour, Ngezahayo's, fence. Ngezahayo was a Tutsi and his house now stood empty. I had already heard that he had been murdered, along with his two sons and wife. His daughter-in-law, Jeane, had been the only one to escape with her life.

Well, I'll just take one of his chickens instead! I thought to myself in a moment of spite. *It's not like that Tutsi needs it any more!*

After killing, skinning and boiling one of Ngezahayo's chickens, I happily feasted on the spoils of my theft. Then I spent the next few hours talking to any remaining villagers I could find.

It was during this time that I learned more information about what had happened to my family. I was told they had become separated while the Army was shooting at them. My sister Christine had not managed to escape with the rest of our family. Instead, some neighbours had helped her travel to my grandparents' house which was just a mile or so away from our home. The village where they lived was also a place where many of my extended family had built their homes.

I will go and see them all before I head to Tanzania, I decided at that moment. *I need to make sure Christine and my grandparents are well.*

I welcomed the comfort of seeing some of my family again. Especially since I had not been in contact with any of my relatives since I left for Tanzania.

If only I had foreseen what would happen the very day I arrived.

4

A Difficult Decision

'Theo – you are here!' Christine exclaimed. 'You have come!'

My sister's face flooded with relief when she caught sight of me arriving at my grandparents' house.

I ran towards her and threw my arms around her. She hugged me back, tightly. My grandfather and grandmother came outside to greet me, too. They were equally happy to see me safe and well.

I couldn't imagine how my sister must have felt when the Army had entered our village. At the tender age of six, she had already seen people shot and killed right in front of her eyes. On top of this, she had suffered the trauma of becoming separated from our parents during the chaos that ensued.

'Did you come for me?' Christine asked, with confused eyes. 'Are you going to take me to Mama and Papa? Do you know where they are?'

I reassured her as best as I could.

'You will be with them soon,' I said. 'Don't be troubled.'

But I knew this was far from the truth.

In reality, I didn't know if either of us would see our parents again and I also believed that I could do little for my sister.

I was adamant that I would proceed to Tanzania, but I was reluctant to take Christine with me. Because of her age,

I couldn't be sure she would survive the journey I had to make. It might have seemed a heartless thought, but I was also afraid she would hamper my attempt to escape and we might both die as a result. I was torn about what to do.

Just as she was too young, my grandparents were too old to flee the country. No one could say what would happen to them if they stayed in Burundi, but this was the sad truth of our current time. The prospect of dying if we stayed or left was a reality for us now. It was just a matter of choosing the less uncertain option.

'Come on, now . . . Sit down, Theo.'

My grandmother's words beckoned me away from my dilemma.

'You must be hungry. I will make you something to eat now.'

As I continued to contemplate taking Christine with me, my grandmother began to prepare a meal of beans and cooked banana. I could smell the delicious aroma as she stirred her cooking pot on the outside stove and it was a welcome distraction. I hadn't eaten a proper meal since I had eaten the chicken the previous afternoon and I felt hungry. My grandfather, Christine and I, brought chairs out into the front yard. We were so excited to see each other again. It had been several months since we had last met and we had much to talk about. As we steered away from topics concerning the war, it almost felt like a normal day, when conflict hadn't existed.

But this feeling wasn't to last long.

My grandmother had just brought us a jug of water to wash our hands with so we could begin our meal, when we heard a noise that made us stop in our tracks.

Tut-tut-tut! Tut-tut-tut!

It was the sound of gunfire. The Army had come!

Our movements were fuelled by instinct.

Without thinking, I leapt up from my chair and looked for a place to run for cover. My grandmother and grandfather were already hurrying into their house to hide. Christine and I started running towards a nearby banana plantation so we could hide ourselves in its tall foliage. But as we joined a swarm of fleeing villagers, the shots started firing closer to us. Christine and I became separated as we changed our course of direction to avoid the shots. I decided to keep running through the fields and finally dropped to the ground in a valley some distance away. My whole body trembling wildly, I looked back towards my grandparents' house. Just two minutes earlier I had been celebrating a reunion with my family. Now what would become of my sister and grandparents? Would they survive the attack?

Should I go back and see? Should I go back and look for Christine?

The task seemed impossible now. It would have been suicidal to return. I almost felt the decision over whether I should bring Christine with me had been taken out of my hands. Even if I waited a day or two and then returned to search for her, would I meet more trouble?

Instead, feeling intense guilt, I made a decision to continue towards Tanzania.

With an extremely heavy heart, I said a silent prayer.

Please God, take care of my sister and my grandparents! Protect them like you have protected me. Spare their lives and let me see them again someday. And be with me as I leave Burundi.

I wondered if I would ever see any of my family again. It was too distressing a prospect to dwell on. I tried to push such thoughts aside.

A three-hour walk away was another village where my father's extended family lived. It was on the way to Tanzania so I decided to stop at my uncle's house. He welcomed me in and gave me a good, hot meal to eat.

That same evening, a relative of his who had been living close to my grandparents' house also arrived to seek refuge at my uncle's home. With him, he brought some news that over-whelmed me with horror. It was an account that caused me immense pain and turmoil.

This relative had also been in the village when the Army had started shooting and had hidden himself in his house. When they had left and he emerged, he had discovered the fate of those who weren't able to take cover so quickly.

'I met your aunt as she was fleeing the village,' he told me. 'Her skin has suffered some serious burns and she is in a bad condition. She told me the Army had caught her, along with four of her children and 18 other members of her family. All of them were women and children. They rounded them up and locked them in a shanty hut. And then they set fire to it. By some miracle she escaped. But she was the only one to get out alive . . . Her four children were burned to death.'

The only one? Her four children burned to death?

Twenty-two members of my aunt's family were dead.

Twenty-two members of *my* family.

These were my aunties and cousins who had been so cruelly murdered. In just a few hours, a large part of my extended fam-ily had been wiped out. The news was too difficult to accept. I was overcome by anger towards their Tutsi murderers. I cursed them loudly over and over again. Part of me yearned for a time when I would be able to take my revenge on the perpetrators.

I questioned God with my agonising thoughts.

Lord, you saved my life – why couldn't you have saved them, too? Why have you let this horror happen to our country? To my family!

Although I felt God had been protecting me as I was fleeing the country, I still did not understand what was happening all around me. Why did he allow such evil to happen? Why did he spare some lives and not others?

I struggled to process the disturbing news I had just received. Though I wanted to cry out and grieve for my relatives, I fought back tears and told myself I would have to mourn their deaths later. I had no stamina left in me to think about the cruel murders or the impact it had just made on my family. Instead, I knew if I was to stay alive, I had to focus on my most immediate need. I had to leave Burundi as fast as I could.

I was now close to the border of Tanzania and faced a huge hurdle. Separating Burundi and Tanzania was a stretch of swampland that would be treacherous to cross. Then, after this point, lay the Malagarasi River. Somehow I would have to get across this as well. Only then would I be safely over the Tanzania border.

Will I ever make it there? I asked myself. *How will I get across the swamp and the river? And what if the Tutsis find me before then . . .*

I uttered another desperate prayer.

Lord, I pleaded, *you have to make a way for me to get to safety in Tanzania. I don't know how you'll do it, but please make a way!*

It would be another prayer the Lord would come to answer in an extraordinary way.

I weighed up my situation. I did not know which route I would have to follow through the swampland to reach the river. I also knew the dangers of getting stuck in the swamp's deep muddy pools which could act like quicksand and easily swallow up a human being. It would be essential to take a route that was safe and had dense plants that could support my weight as I walked across their roots. After that, I was hoping there would be boats available to ferry me to Tanzania. I had never learned how to swim so that wasn't an option.

I spent the next two days wandering around my uncle's village and talking to people.

Was anyone else attempting to make it across the border? If they were, did they know a good route to get there? Did anyone know the best way to cross the swamp and the river?

Eventually I found someone willing to help me. He was a Hutu Burundian who lived in Tanzania. He had crossed back to the country to help take some of his family over with him.

'When we all leave, you can follow us,' he told me. 'I know a good path to get there. I will bring you to a point where there is also a canoe to take you across the river.'

It was a relief to find someone who was confident we could get to Tanzania safely. However, the journey wouldn't be so straightforward.

'We cannot cross over during the day,' he added. 'The Army keeps watch over the swamp when there's light. Be prepared to meet us at night when we will travel.'

Just the thought of crossing the swamp made me extremely anxious. But to travel at night was all the more frightening. We would have to take extra care of where we stepped. One wrong foot could risk us slipping into the mud and being dragged underneath the swamp.

That same night, I met with the man and his family, ready to begin our journey. We travelled by moonlight, all of us terrified about what lay ahead of us. We weren't the only ones crossing that night. In the dark I could make out hundreds of other silhouettes which must have been other Hutus who had the same intentions as us. I had become part of a mass exodus.

Reaching the swamp, I followed the steps of the family I had met as best as I could. I could see two or three people in front of me and perhaps the same number behind me, and to my left and right. But my main focus was on placing my feet in the right spots, firmly grounded on the roots of solid swamp plants. The path we were following seemed to have a good number of bushes to walk across. The trip across the swamp should have taken a couple of hours, but since we were walking so cautiously, it would take us about eight. During this time, scores of giant mosquitoes nipped at our skin and feasted on our blood. I swatted them away, knowing many would be carrying malaria.

We progressed making little sound except the squelching and thuds of our feet as we walked and the whispers between families trying to stay together or direct each other to make cautious steps. Around us the mosquitoes and swamp insects buzzed loudly in our ears. Then, once in a while, we would hear an alarming scream. They were always similar refrains.

'The Army. The Army! They are coming! They are chasing after us!'

My heart would skip a beat at these reports and we would all stand as still as we could, rooted to our spots. Was it true? Was the Army chasing us? Would they start shooting at any minute?

Thankfully, no sound of shooting came and the cries eventually died down.

I would hear murmurs in the dark.

'They are just dreaming!'

'This war has driven people crazy.'

'It is just hallucinations. The Army would be foolish to follow us here.'

And so we continued our sluggish trek. The sun had begun to rise by the time we recognised the reflection of its light on the plane of water ahead of us. We had reached the River Malagarasi. At this point, I had lost the family I was meant to be following, but since there were so many others travelling, it hadn't been hard to end up by the river's side.

I spotted a very small canoe in the water and saw a line of people waiting to board it.

I was truly elated to have made it through the swamp.

I am still alive! I thought. *It won't be long until I can get into the boat and then I will be safe in Tanzania. The worst part of my trip is over!*

I had no idea of how wrong I was.

As the boat glided closer to the shore, I observed its simple construction. It was tiny and made from two halves of a tree trunk bound with rope. A small man used a single wooden oar to push it along. It took 20 minutes for him to ferry his passengers along, one at a time, as the boat was so small. I said a prayer of thanks that I had found the Burundian francs at my father's house. Now I had something to pay the boatman with for my ride.

I must have waited for two hours before it was finally my turn to board.

But when the boatman saw me, he shook his head frantically.

'Oh no!' he fussed when he realised I was next in line. 'It is not possible!'

'What?' I said, confused. 'What's not possible?'

'Too heavy, too heavy . . .' he raved, waving his hand up and down to indicate my frame.

'I don't understand . . .' I said. 'Are you saying I'm too heavy to take?'

As he finished his sentence, his words hit me like a blow.

He said: 'Yes, you can't come with me. You're too heavy. If I take you, my boat is going to sink!'

5

In the Forest

I felt like I had just leapt from a high mountain edge and was waiting to hit the ground.

My life depended on making the river crossing, yet here I was facing the prospect that I might not even make it into the boat.

It was true I was not a small man. I was almost six feet and weighed maybe 80 kilos (12½ stone). After everything I had been through in the past week, how could I have imagined a simple wooden canoe would leave me hanging in a balance between life and death?

Behind me lay the treacherous swamp and images of the Army waiting with tanks and guns to shoot me dead. Ahead of me lay the dreary depths of the River Malagarasi, ready to rush into my lungs and drown me.

My hope was extinguished. Which death would be easier?

'Is there no way to take me?' I pleaded.

I brought out my Burundian francs.

'I have enough money to pay you well,' I said. 'Please, you cannot leave me here!'

The boatman saw my notes and didn't take too long to think.

'Well, if you want to,' he said. 'I will try to take you. But I cannot promise the boat won't go under. If it does, be prepared to swim.'

Swim?

I was fairly sure I would drown if I hit the water. But what choice did I have? I couldn't trek back over the swamp to return to the killing fields of Burundi. I needed to cross the river to reach Tanzania and secure the only chance of survival I believed I had left.

Lord, please keep the boat afloat! I prayed. *You've protected my life so far. Now, save me from drowning!*

'I'm ready to take the chance. I have no other choice,' I told the boatman, though in truth I felt almost paralysed with fear.

I sat down in the bottom of the canoe, legs stretched out in front of me. The boatman was perched on the top ledge behind me. As he began to push us away from the shore, I confessed to him that I couldn't swim.

'Don't worry,' he told me. 'If we sink, I will try to save you.'

He was a petite man and I wondered if he really could.

As the boat glided along, the boatman's prediction came true.

His canoe's construction was poor and water started to seep in at the back where the two tree trunk halves met. I felt the seat of my trousers become wet. The boatman addressed the alarm in my eyes.

'Yes, we are sinking,' he told me. 'But don't be afraid. I will help you swim the rest of the way.'

'But I am too heavy for you,' I said, horror rising in my chest. 'How will you carry me?'

'Please – stay calm,' he replied. 'You will go under the water and will struggle for a while. But if you pass out and stop struggling, I will be able to carry your weight and swim with you.'

So the boatman was sincere about wanting to save me. But I would have to be almost dead before he could try.

The seriousness of my predicament was overwhelming. The boat was sinking and it was likely I was going to drown.

Water continued to pour into the canoe, soaking my trousers. Panic engulfed me as it rose, slowly reaching my lap.

Suddenly the weight was too much. The entire canoe tipped over. It threw us out into the murky water.

I thrashed about, kicking my legs, flailing my arms to reach for any anchor I could find. I gasped and choked, swallowing water which stung my nose and throat.

This was it! I was drowning.

Then my fingers brushed against something solid. Somehow I managed to reach out and lock my fingers around it. It felt like the branch of a tree. I pulled myself towards it and felt my chest hit something firm. It seemed to be a dense collection of branches and plant roots. They had meshed together and were floating in the water like a natural raft.

I grabbed hold of the mass with both hands and hoisted my chest above water level. It was strong enough to hold my weight.

Coughing and spluttering, I gasped for air.

When I turned around, I saw the boatman struggling with his capsized canoe. He finally succeeded in tipping it over again and climbed back inside.

He called out to where I was: 'I am coming. Keep holding on!'

Within minutes, he had reached my side and held out his hand to help me back in again.

Overcome with shock, I sat in the canoe, hyperventilating as I tried to regain my breath.

I was too stunned to even worry about what might happen next, now that I was back inside the canoe.

'You are okay,' the boatman said, trying to ease my distress. 'You are alive, you will be fine.'

He paddled rapidly, eager for us to reach the other side of the river. But, just as before, my weight was too much for the vessel and water began to seep in again.

The banks of the river we were headed towards were now within sight, but I doubted we would make it there before the canoe flooded once more.

This nightmare is endless, I thought to myself. *I have no chance. I will go under the water again!*

The water climbed towards my lap again and I braced myself for the canoe to overturn. This time I doubted I would be so lucky as to find anything to hold onto.

Then, just as the canoe started to tip and sway with the load of the water, the boatman urged me loudly: 'Don't panic! You will not drown. We are close to the bank and the water isn't deep.'

As he said this, the canoe fell onto its side. It threw us into the water again. I scrambled to regain my balance and thrust my feet towards the ground.

Thank you, Lord!

Standing up, the waters reached my chest.

Thank you, Lord! I am safe!

I am safe now!

The banks of the river were only a few metres away. I couldn't believe I had made it across. The boatman was also on his feet and had grabbed onto the canoe to pull it along. I helped him drag it as we waded towards the river's side.

Once on dry land, I fought to recover my breath and my nerves.

I had almost drowned. I nearly hadn't made it.

I was tempted to lie down and rest on the ground for a while, but fear urged me to keep moving. I managed to thank the boatman for taking me and caring for my safety, before he hurried to pick up more passengers.

'You are lucky,' he told me before he left. 'Those branches and roots were never there before. The storm we had a few days ago must have washed them into the river. It is a good thing or you might have lost your life.'

Never there before? Had I heard him right?

Was it really a matter of luck?

It did seem like I had been the luckiest man to have escaped as many dangers as I had during my flight from Burundi. I was sure if I told people, they would not believe the events I described. Even I struggled to believe so much had happened to me in such a short space of time. But in my eyes, these fortunate interventions weren't the product of luck. Instead I saw them as nothing short of miraculous and the act of a powerful God. In every situation where I had faced death and felt like I had no hope, God had somehow moved to spare my life in an incredible way. Surely he had placed the branches and roots in the river for me. Surely he was watching over me.

But why? I thought. *Why has he done these things?*

I believed God loved me just as he did all his children. But it was hard to comprehend why he seemed to be protecting me while others were dying.

And how could I imagine he would continue to do such awesome things?

Though I didn't know it at the time, the truth was that he would.

At that moment, after crossing the border of Burundi and leaving its blood-hungry conflict behind me, I might have allowed myself to imagine for a moment that the worst of my troubles were over. In fact, now that I was in Tanzania, they had really just begun.

There was no border control. There were no guards or troops positioned to stop illegal entries. There was no one waiting to send me back now that I had arrived on Tanzanian soil.

It was the biggest relief to have made it across the border.

However, what I was faced with now was a barrier of thick, uncultivated brush and forest trees which would be hard to penetrate.

Thankfully, I soon realised this wouldn't prove a problem.

I spotted a narrow path that had already been cleared through the trees and overgrown plants. It had likely been made by other escaping Burundians who had brought tools like sickles and knives with them during their flight. I followed this opening, eager to get as far away from the Burundian border as possible. Though it was a relief to be on foreign soil now, I remembered stories circulated from the last civil war about the Burundian Army's tenacity for hunting their escaping countrymen. Several soldiers had endured the challenges of the swamp and river crossing to follow their victims over the Tanzanian border so they could continue with their hateful massacring. Even neutral Tanzanians had been murdered during the pursuit of Hutus who were running away.

As I walked, the slippery mud below my feet became firm and dry. This, along with an increase in the number of trees, let me know I was entering forestland now. Sounds of wildlife and the rustling of greenery by wild pigs and rabbits were welcome signs of life to detect.

I eventually found other Burundians travelling in the forest, too. Though we were all strangers, there seemed to be an unspoken solidarity among us. After all, we were in the same boat, sharing each other's desperation and fight for survival. I was certain we were all equally exhausted from our journey across the border, equally traumatised from what we had seen of the war and equally afraid and unsure about what lay ahead for us.

It wasn't long before I felt weak with hunger and thirst. The only things I had brought across the border with me were the clothes I was wearing and the few Burundian francs left in my pocket. I gratefully accepted when a man who was travelling with his wife and two kids held out his water can towards me and handed me some of their meal of potatoes and beans. He had spotted me taking a rest on the ground and could see I carried nothing with me. His generosity wasn't unusual. Several other refugees had brought food with them or carried jerry cans of water. If any of them sat down to eat or took out their water, they offered what they had to those around them. It astounded and touched me that my fellow countrymen were still willing to share what little they had left, especially when they didn't know where their next meal or supply of water would come from.

My journey further into Tanzania continued but extreme exhaustion hit me after just a few hours. I must have been walking in my sleep as it was only when I felt my body collide with a tree that I finally gave into my fatigue. I dropped to the ground right next to the tree and slept deeply.

I woke to the sound of voices talking around me.

Where was I?

I opened my eyes and sat up. Tall trees stood to attention in every direction.

Yes, I was in the Tanzania forest now!

The voices belonged to other Burundians. Many more seemed to have joined the trail previous travellers had flattened out in the forest. Some sat on the ground, huddled together, eating or resting. Others were still passing in groups along the route. I noted how easily they talked, without lowered voices, an indication that they felt safer now they were further away from the border.

I felt an urge to get up quickly and continue walking but then the irony of the situation hit me. Here we all were, earnestly following this trail, but none of us really knew where it would lead. Where were we really going? Would we find anyone willing to give us food and shelter when we reached its end? How long would we have to stay here in Tanzania? And what if we continued walking and found nothing – what would we do then?

That same day, speaking to another refugee in the forest, one who had been in the forest for some weeks but had come back along the path to find his family, I discovered the answers to some of my questions.

'There are no aid agencies here or charities for refugees,' he told me. 'There really is no one here to help us.'

It was a crippling discovery.

What then would happen to us? Who could we turn to?

We will all die of hunger in no time, I thought. *We have no hope!*

I hadn't been prepared to hear this. What would I do now?

Even with this knowledge, I felt there was nothing else I could do except to keep moving. As I travelled inland, a few isolated fields appeared. At first, the Tanzanian farmers tending them had been willing to offer food and help to the Burundians they saw, but by the time I arrived, their kindness had turned to frustration and anger because they felt overwhelmed by our numbers. By the number of people I saw in the forest with me, I guessed there could have been a few thousand Burundian refugees.

There really was no one then to give us food, healthcare or a roof over our heads. Though the forest was a place where only wild animals and plants could survive, it would now be our home until an alternative came along. And as long as we stayed here, most of us would be in a desperate search for the food and water we needed for our survival.

Some smart Burundians had brought hunting dogs with them. Others had brought cooking pots and a bag of grain to sustain them for a few weeks.

For Burundians like me who had nothing with them, we were thankful to discover it was a good time of the year when the forest yielded wild fruit and roots which helped fill our stomachs. I ate *amasarasi*, with its sweet yellow flesh, and *intabataba*, a fruit that looks similar to coffee beans. I also happened upon some cassava and a white hard root called *inanka*. At times, we were forced to help ourselves to the produce from some of the small unattended fields we came across, mainly banana, bean, cassava and maize plantations. Previously I could never have imagined taking something from someone that wasn't mine to take. But in our predicament, how could we think twice about doing what we needed to survive?

For water, we found forest streams which we continuously returned to. If it rained, we would happily drink from a rain puddle or other stagnant collections, no matter how green or pungent they were. Most of my conversations with other Burundians would be about where we might find water or something to eat.

When night fell, the only place to sleep was the bare forest ground. If someone had built a fire, people gravitated towards it as the temperature would drop dramatically at night and few had extra clothing or blankets with them. There was no real shelter apart from the trees. If it rained, we got soaked through. We were aware there were snakes meandering around us as we slept, but they were the least of our worries. I slept in the same shirt and trousers. I owned nothing else. I was sure I smelt badly by now and ticks had started to crawl over my skin and in my hair, constantly nipping at me. I felt worthless and cheap, as if I had reached my lowest form of existence. Yet I got used to feeling this way.

Since we refugees realised there was nowhere to go, we started organising ourselves inside the forest. It was a trend that we congregated into like-minded groups. One family would join another family to huddle together, and members of the same village or community formed their own gatherings. At times, I found a couple of other young students like myself to sleep close to or go scavenging for food and water with. During others, I travelled alone in the forest.

My day would follow a typical course. On waking, my first priority would be to search for food – usually any fruit or root I could find. I'd locate a water source to drink from and then my next priority would be to obtain information. I would approach other Burundians I met with two main objectives in mind. Firstly, I wanted to find out if they had heard news or rumours of any place where we could find more food or aid of any sort. Secondly, I gave out the names of my family and friends who had fled Burundi. I still hoped I would be reunited with the loved ones I had become separated from. During that time, many of those I met would also describe how they had ended up in the Tanzanian forest. I heard countless stories of escape and survival. Stories of fear, desperation and witnessing horrific acts. Stories of loss and tragedy. My heart bled for my people and for what we had suffered – and for what we were still going through.

Depending on information I received about where food might be found, or a relative or friend located, I continued to move around in the forest.

A few weeks after I had arrived in the forest, it became clear to me there were three small villages close by that most refugees were headed towards: Kigadrye, Heru-Ushingo and Gitanga. These villages were rumoured to have clinics and schools for refugees.

'Life will be better there,' some people said. 'The Tanzanians have facilities to help us.'

Others warned of the tribulations we were likely to encounter.

'Too many Burundians are headed there,' someone warned me. 'I don't know how they are finding food. You'd be foolish to join them.'

But I had to make a decision. In the end I made it based on one thing: I needed to know what had happened to my family.

Going to one of the villages would give me a chance to gather more information from people who might have seen them. There was even a chance I might find some of them there.

I will take the risk, I thought. *It is worth finding them.*

I decided I would head to the nearest village of He-ru-Ushingo, which was a 20-mile walk away.

I began my journey and that same day found out something I had longed to know.

I couldn't believe it when I ran into someone I recognised from my home village in Burundi. He told me he had just left Heru-Ushingo and then he gave me some news I had been praying to hear.

Could this really be true? I thought to myself as I listened to my friend's words.

'I have just seen your mother and father and siblings in Heru-Ushingo,' he said. 'They are alive and well! They are living there in a shelter they built.'

My heart almost burst with a joy I had not felt in a very long time.

They are alive! They are really alive and all together! Thank you, Lord!

6

Together Again

Arriving in Heru-Ushingo, I could tell earlier warnings about what I might find had been accurate. The village, which was populated by roughly a hundred Tanzanian families, had now become inundated with Burundian refugees. I estimated there could have been more than a hundred thousand of us there. What didn't prove true were the reports about the existence of a school or medical clinic to help these refugees. There was just one primary school that served Tanzanian students and the only medical facility was a tiny and ill-equipped dispensary. With the Tanzanians living there being overwhelmed by our numbers and equally wanting nothing to do with us, we weren't much better off living in the village than we had been deep in the forest.

The refugees retreated to the outskirts of Heru-Ushingo, creating makeshift shelters. It was an overwhelming sight to witness the sheer number of them.

The Tanzanians became even more disturbed when the refugees started to pose a threat to their lives. For as they congregated together, diseases began to spread quickly. Because of the absence of adequate shelter, sanitation and medical facilities, illnesses like malaria and food poisoning were common.

Prevalent above them all was a disease that started to kill dozens every day: dysentery.

On the outskirts of the village, it was a daily occurrence to see families mourning over a loved-one who had succumbed to the effects of dysentery. They carried their deceased further out, away from the refugee shelters, dug shallow holes in the ground, and laid their relatives to rest there. When too many bodies were buried in the same area, an overpowering smell would stain the air and the refugees would pack up and settle elsewhere in the forest.

With thousands of refugees crammed together in limited space, the Tanzanian village of Heru-Ushingo was now an ideal breeding ground for dysentery. I could see many of those who'd already settled there had become ill from this condition. It was a predicament that almost made me want to turn back into the forest had it not been for the incredible news I had just received about my family being there. I was determined not to leave until I found them.

The same day I arrived in Heru-Ushingo, as I was speaking to other Burundians, I was given some advice: 'There is a group of boys who are students like you. They are living over by the pineapple plantation. Go and join them.'

I hoped to find a few friends I might recognise from among them, so I took the advice and wandered over to the plantation. Beside it was the small primary school and the owner had generously offered up one of its rooms as a shelter for the refugees. There were more than fifteen boys gathered together, so not everyone managed to fit into the small room to sleep. The rest would sleep on the hay that was piled between the soil rows of the pineapple plantation.

Since it was already approaching evening, I decided to spend my first night in the village with these boys. The following day,

I planned to begin the search for my parents and siblings. I could hardly wait to be reunited with them.

The next morning, I set off in the direction of the shelters where my friend had described I would find my family. Though at first I could only make out a disorderly collection of grass huts, with most of its inhabitants sitting outside, it didn't take me too long to spot them. Within minutes, my eyes were fixed on two figures I recognised well, even from a distance.

'Mama! Papa!' I called out as I hurried towards my parents. 'I've found you!'

You would have thought we'd cry tears of happiness at being reunited again. But there were no tears shed as I embraced my startled parents. We were all so traumatised by our experiences, it was hard for anything to stir our emotions. Instead, we gathered together, patting each other's backs and smiling broadly that we were together again. I could spot the relief deep in my parents' eyes.

My siblings – Normand, Nixon, Didavine, Imelde and Onesime – were also with my parents. Only Christine remained missing.

'I can't believe you are here!' my father exclaimed.

He pointed to the space in front of the hut they were standing outside. 'Come, let us all sit down here. You must rest and tell us how you are, Theo.'

'How did you get to Tanzania?'

'Who did you come with?'

'How did you find us?'

'Are you keeping well?'

We had so many questions to ask each other as my eyes examined the faces of my family and I watched theirs examine mine.

To find most of my immediate family alive and safe in Tanzania had been one of my deepest desires. Yet, at the same time, I couldn't help feeling a profound sense of sadness. My mother, father and siblings didn't look well. Their clothes were torn and filthy and they had become emaciated through lack of food. Their faces were etched with a dejection that seemed to have aged them by years. It was a hard sight to take in. I wondered how much they had suffered and endured since the last time we had been together, just three months back.

My father had managed to build a grass hut for his family – the one I had found them in front of. It had been made from a skeleton of strong twigs and branches tied together, then laced with strands of dry grass.

Catching a glimpse inside, I could see it was empty, save for a pile of clothes and a couple of cooking pots on the ground. Although I could tell their shelter was the best one standing in the collection of huts around us – my father's sense of pride never failing even in such circumstances – my mind kept seeing images of my family's comfortable home back in Burundi. The comparison with the tiny makeshift hut they now lived in was heart-breaking to me. They had lost everything. I had never wanted to see my family this way.

My father's voice interrupted my thoughts. 'You must tell us how you came, Theo,' he said. 'We had been so worried about you.'

'Yes, I will share everything with you,' I told my parents and siblings as they sat huddled around me. 'God saved my life so many times. You may not even believe that I am still here. It is by a series of miracles that I am alive and have found you all again . . .'

We sat talking for a long time outside my family's hut. I recounted the story of my escape from Burundi. My family uttered praises to God when they heard how my life had been incredibly spared.

I also told them about finding Christine at my grandparents' house, but how I had to leave her to journey on alone when the Army had chased us. Even then, my deep sense of guilt at not having returned to find her weighed heavily on me.

Now we had been reunited as a family, her absence was felt by us all and it was painful. In part, we were all silently mourning her. We wanted to keep hoping she was alive and that she would find us somehow. But wasn't that too big a hope? I kept up a constant prayer in my heart that we would see her again.

Lord, please bring Christine back to us. You can do this for us . . . somehow . . .

My father began to tell me how my family had managed to flee to Tanzania. He revealed he had left our village, by himself, the same day the President had been kidnapped. Those to be murdered first were always the leaders or heads of communities so as to cripple any formations of power, and my father was an influential person in ours. He had taken a *panga* (a bladed African tool) with him and had actually been one of the refugees who had helped to shape the route in the forest that I had been able to follow once I landed in Tanzania. My mother and five of my siblings had then fled after the Army targeted our village with tanks to take revenge on the Hutus there. This is when they had become separated from Christine. They had been helped to the Tanzanian border by other fleeing Burundians – once again ready to care for their fellow brothers and sisters.

Normand had actually been on an Army base when the President's coup occurred. He had fled immediately and had somehow managed to find my family as they travelled through the Tanzanian forest.

'We must praise God we are back together!' my mother exclaimed, using what little energy she had left in her spirit to try to comfort us all. 'Let us not forget to thank him!'

We couldn't ignore the wretched condition we had been reduced to. Yet, even in the face of everything, my family were united in our feelings of deep gratitude to God. We found it hard to doubt that his mercies had been with us even through the traumatic events we had seen and experienced. Deep down, I was certain we also shared the belief that death was only around the corner for us all. However, we still praised God for keeping most of our family together.

I handed my parents the money which remained from the amount I had found in my father's pair of socks. I hadn't spent much of it yet as there had been nowhere to purchase food in the forest. Now we were in a village, we would be able to use it for some time to sustain us. It was yet another reason for us to thank God.

That day, my family told me about another of his mercies that had come to their aid – one that meant they were able to eat even though they could not afford to. It was in the form of a Catholic Burundian priest called Father Bazeduka. I was amazed when I heard about what he had been doing for my people.

Father Bazeduka's arrival into Heru-Ushingo was announced by the vibrating motors of two vehicles approaching the refugee plots.

Riding in a separate car, he brought with him a truck loaded with bags of maize. At the first hint of his arrival, people suddenly stopped what they were doing to form an orderly group as the truck halted close to the settlement of shelters.

Father Bazeduka was a Burundian priest who worked in Tanzania. He must have been in his mid-30s. Dressed in black, with the traditional white clerical collar, he had a kind but plain face. Appearance-wise, he wouldn't have stood out from other Burundians, but his actions certainly set him apart.

I never found out more about Father Bazeduka, except to observe he seemed to be working on his own, accompanied by a few hired workers. He had carefully organised his methods of distribution so that representatives of a collection of ten shelters would receive the maize needed for their members. This avoided any desperate grabbing or fighting for food when he visited. Father Bazeduka would enter the village every day, sometimes up to three times, to bring in and store the grain he was distributing. Then, after every two days, he would allow it to be handed out. It was the only source of food the Heru-Ushingo refugees could be certain of. In fact, Father Bazeduka was the only source of help that came to the refugees. Though a lone figure, I wonder if he saw just how vital his act of charity and love was to us all.

Before I found them, my parents and siblings had been sustaining themselves with the maize he brought. A staple in the Burundian diet, the maize was unground and dry. Since those who received it had nothing to grind it with, they would simply boil the grain and eat it without salt. It had no taste whatsoever, but this food was essential to their survival. I knew I would always be thankful to Father Bazeduka for what he had done for my family and my people. His lone act of charity must have saved thousands of lives.

I had been reunited with my parents but I still returned to my community of students each night after visiting them. In Burundian culture, I was of an age where it would not have been appropriate to continue to live with them. I also felt I did not want to burden them. I shared the grain distributed to our group of students and borrowed cooking pans from other refugees when we needed to boil it. We continued to live together and help each other with day-to-day activities like scavenging for food or collecting water from the dirty river which ran next to Heru-Ushingo. Once or twice a week, we would go there to wash ourselves, too. I would take off my trousers and shirt, the only clothes I had, and attempt to scrub the grime out of them without the use of soap. Then we would wait by the river until our clothes were dry.

And so we continued our existence. Our lives were suspended in an uncertain limbo.

Days passed, yet we did not really know what we were sustaining ourselves for. Would any aid agencies arrive to give us a better quality of life? Or were we destined to die unnoticed before long?

The sight of dead bodies being carried away for disposal had become familiar. We were sure it was inevitable we would all succumb to the same fate soon. Death from disease seemed moments away.

Having been in the village for just a few weeks, I ran into members of my extended family, as well as a few friends and neighbours whom I had known in Burundi. Like us, they had come to settle in the land in and around Heru-Ushingo. But my joy at seeing them safe would turn to despair as some fell ill and died. One neighbour from my home village, named Masunzu, had escaped with his wife and seven young children. But within three weeks of their arrival into Heru-Ushingo, one of his children contracted dysentery. Just a week later, it had taken hold of another four of his children. Masunzu and his wife's anguish was unspeakable as they buried five of their children in the Tanzanian forest. Because of this, Masunzu decided to take his wife and remaining two children back to Burundi –

preferring the risk of murder by Tutsis over the threat of death by dysentery.

Lord! I would cry out in my prayers. *What is happening? Why are you letting us see such pain and tragedy? It is too much to bear.*

The irony was that as many Burundian refugees were dying in Tanzania as were being murdered back in Burundi. We had simply exchanged one death sentence for another.

My need to cry out to God and find some comfort from him was so huge, I and some of my fellow Christian students found a local Tanzanian Pentecostal church we could attend every Sunday. In a strange way, although our current circumstances were desperate, I was still extremely grateful for all I believed God had done for me. After all, thus far, he had protected me and my family and displayed his power in an incredible way. Part of me was drawn to church just to praise God and feel closer to him.

I believed he could hear my prayers and could answer them if he willed. Would he? I did not know. But I knew I still had to pray.

And so, each Sunday, though still in the same stained and dirty shirt and trousers I had worn months back when I arrived in Tanzania, I sat myself down at the back of the church with several of my student friends. As time passed, I offered to sing during the service, too, urged on by a part of me which wanted to serve God in any way I could.

The service would be held in Kiha, a language close to the Burundian language Kirundi, so we were able to understand most of what was being said. The Tanzanian church-goers didn't seem to mind visiting refugees so much, or perhaps they were just overwhelmed by our presence and felt helpless to pro-test. Though some would greet us or smile, none would ven-ture so far as to volunteer help or aid. I was sure the majority of the congregation were afraid of associating too closely with us because of their fears of catching disease.

Sitting on the mud floor of the church, which was small and had no chairs, I would lift up my hands to God as I prayed.

Lord, save me and my family from disease and death.

Keep us safe and return my sister Christine to us, too.

Heal our country and stop the war. Make a way for us to return to our homeland.

And Lord, I pray that I might even go back to school again one day. I want to have a future.

Yes, these were big requests but they were my deepest desires. The likelihood was that me and all my family might be dead within a few months, for we were surviving on a diet of maize and little else and had no means of protecting ourselves against the onslaught of dysentery that was fast claiming lives.

Surely, I reasoned, if my God was so big, there was nothing that could stop him from answering my prayers?

However, what little hope I still clung onto soon dissipated when, just a few weeks after being reunited with my parents, something I had most feared happened.

Arriving to visit my family, I found my father lying on the floor of their grass hut. It was unusual for him to be taking a nap during the day, so I knew something was wrong.

'Father,' I said. 'Why are you lying down? What is the matter?'

As he lifted his head to look me in the eyes, I should have known what his reply would be even before he had uttered it. Even so, I still felt like I had been painfully wounded when he finally spoke up.

'Theo,' he said. 'I am sick. I have dysentery.'

7

Disease and Death

The village of Heru-Ushingo had one dispensary. But it was of little use to us as it had no medicines for treating dysentery such as rehydration salts or antibiotics. Painkillers were the only comfort it could offer. What the dispensary did have, however, was a public toilet. Every day, up to fifty people queued outside the ragged hut which concealed a deep hole in the ground. It was almost certain that at least half of the people waiting to use this public toilet had already contracted dysentery. The wait was so long, many often left the line after soiling themselves before they could take their turn.

It was this line that my father now joined well over fifteen times a day, each time bearing less strength to endure the long wait.

Being a disease spread through contaminated water and food, it was no surprise that dysentery was rife among the refugees. The water we used to drink or cook our maize with was often contaminated, deriving from the river where we would also wash ourselves and any soiled clothes. We tried hard to keep our living areas clean. If we weren't able to use the dispensary toilet, we would go out into the forest, away from the settlements, to relieve ourselves on the ground. It might have been ideal to dig and create more holes in the ground to keep our living conditions sanitary, but we lacked the tools to make such things.

Little acts of hygiene like washing our hands often were pointless when the water we used to wash them with was already contaminated.

And then there were the flies that were drawn to our clothes, skin, food and waste like magnets. These hastened the spread of the disease, especially since each of us must have been covered by at least fifty flies at any one time.

A refugee without access to antibiotics and rehydration fluids would almost certainly die once they contracted dysentery. The bacterial disease of the intestines produced painful cramps, fever and the passing of diarrhoea with mucus and blood. After a couple of weeks or so, it was inevitable they would succumb to death by dehydration.

As I looked at my father lying on the dirt floor of his hut, I felt unbearable distress.

He is going to die! I am going to lose my papa!

It was sure to be a matter of days before the disease claimed his life. My family and I would be helpless to do anything but watch him grow weaker and weaker.

Then we heard a rumour that gave us a ray of hope.

'They are saying there is a mission hospital 25 miles away in a village called Shunga,' a neighbour told us. 'If your papa is strong enough to walk, send him there. It is your only hope.'

Father agreed to go. There was no way he would survive if he didn't. He went along with other members of our family we had reunited with, and who were also ill – my uncle's wife and a cousin of mine with three children who all had dysentery.

If the rumour was true, there was a chance they could all be cured before it was too late.

Lord, did you bring us here to die? I anguished. *Are you going to answer any of the prayers I have lifted up to you?*

As Papa set off on his journey, with barely enough strength left to keep him upright as he walked, I knew it might be the last time I saw him alive.

Now an even heavier sadness descended upon my family. Papa's absence was another reminder to us that our chances of survival were small indeed.

Not long afterwards, an unexpected ray of light suddenly pierced our dejection. Someone arrived at the pineapple plantation to tell me some news.

I wasn't sure if I should believe it or not but, just the same, I raced to my parents' hut to find out for myself.

When I got there, I blinked in disbelief at what I was seeing. Was she really alive? Had she really found us?

'Is that you?' I called out. 'Is that really you?'

Standing, clinging to my mother's waist was my sister Christine.

The figure I saw was dirty and unkempt, and she looked pale and depleted, but here was Christine alive and with us! I resisted the urge to break down into a flood of tears. My guilt at having separated from my sister, and the relief that she was alive, brought a strong wave of emotion over me. I had been convinced Christine had been killed and I believed I would never be able to forgive myself for not taking her with me.

Thank you Lord! I cried out in my heart. *It's a miracle Christine is here!*

God had answered this prayer of mine – one I had desperately craved. Now I felt immense gratitude.

'How did you get here?' I asked Christine. 'Where are *Nyokuru* (Grandma) and *Sokuru* (Grandpa)?'

'I don't know,' she told me. 'When the Army started shooting at us, I never went back to their house. Instead, I followed some other Hutus who were running to Tanzania. They helped me come through the swamp and get across the river. Strangers looked after me. They shared their food with me and gave me water to drink when they saw that I was alone. I kept asking them if they knew where you all were but no one did. Then, one day, some of our old neighbours saw me. They said they had seen Mama and Papa and they brought me here.'

To me, Christine's arrival was another miracle. Here was a six-year-old who had managed to escape the genocide and flee her country with only the kindness of strangers to help her. And now she had located us among thousands of other refugees.

I was touched once again by the humanity of my fellow countrymen. Though in such desperate circumstances, and lacking resources themselves, they had saved the life of my sister though their kindness. They had fed her, taken her into their care and even used their own money to send her across the Malagarasi River. *No one could ever be so poor as to not be able to help a fellow brother or sister,* I thought.

Inevitably, Christine had been traumatised by what she had witnessed of the war and during her journey to Tanzania. But it was a comfort that she was back with us.

I couldn't stop praising God for what he had done for our family – for sparing Christine's life and bringing her safely to us. Was this a sign that he had been listening to my prayers and that he was able to answer them all?

Just a couple of days after Christine had arrived, my attention was diverted to a more urgent question, one that involved my health.

I had awoken to the feeling of severe cramps in my stomach.

What was the matter? I felt an urgent need to relieve myself.

Running outside, I hurried to join the queue at the dispensary's toilet hut.

A few hours later, after several more painful cramps and visits to relieve myself, I realised what was happening. There was blood in my stools and I couldn't ignore what this meant. I knew it was a matter of time before I fell ill; the reality of what was happening was frightening.

Now I had contracted dysentery, too.

The disintegration of my health was rapid. Within a couple of days, I found myself weaker than I'd ever felt before. The symptoms of the dysentery were relentless. Every ounce of strength seemed to be leaving my body and there was nothing I could do. Without access to clean water or rehydration salts, I was dehydrating fast.

I will die very soon, I thought. *I should go and stay with Mama now.*

Light-headed and staggering, I carried myself over to my family's hut, where I collapsed on the floor of their shelter.

Mama attended to me the best she could, praying over me and feeding me what little she had. It pained me even more to see her despair. But we all knew what was coming.

Just a day later, I was too weak to even take myself outside to defecate. Instead I relieved myself where I was. All hope had left me. I was just waiting for death to carry me away.

As I lay there, I knew I had to make my peace with God. But I still had so many unanswered questions that disturbed me.

Why had God protected me so many times before, only to let me die like this?

Why had no one come to help us refugees? Why had we been allowed to suffer and live in such appalling conditions?

I still felt waves of anger towards those I held responsible for my predicament: the Burundian Army, my former Tutsi neighbours who had killed my Hutu friends, the powerful countries who were doing nothing to stop what was happening in Burundi.

I wished I could forgive those I felt hatred towards before I died. As a Christian who recognised my own sinfulness and who was grateful for God's saving grace, I knew it was important. Yet, I couldn't bring myself to let go of my anger.

Though I believed in God and knew he was supposed to be good, I wished I could understand why he had allowed everything to happen the way it had.

My prayer for survival was as feeble as I felt.

Lord, will you let me live? Will you let me get better?

Would God save me again? Did he really care enough?

Just a couple of days after I had arrived at my parents' hut, my questions were answered.

As I lay drifting in and out of consciousness, I heard footsteps approaching me.

'Theo, wake up! Wake up!' the voices said. 'They are looking for students. Get up!'

Pairs of hands reached over to grab me under my shoulders. They clutched at my head and limbs. Then I felt myself being lifted up. I was being carried way.

Where were they taking me?

'You're going to a hospital,' I heard someone say. 'They wanted students. You've been chosen.'

What was I hearing?

I was carried to a large pick-up truck that was parked a few hundred metres away. There were already three young men and one young lady inside the canopied storage. All of them were sitting up against the sides, except for one boy who was lying down on the metal floor behind the driver's cabin.

I lay down on the floor, too, unable to hold myself up. Then a white man in his 30s appeared and said something I couldn't understand to the people who had brought me there. After this, he climbed into the cabin, started the engine and began to drive us away.

Who is this man and where did he come from? I thought. *Is he really taking us to a hospital?*

It was obvious that every one of us in the truck was very ill from dysentery. I was familiar with a few of the boys with me. The young man lying on the floor was called Havyarimana and he was four years younger than me. I recognised him as he was someone who had lived in the same village as my parents.

The drive was horrendous. We bumped and slid around on the hard metal, hitting our heads on the walls as the truck navigated uneven paths. Havyarimana kept vomiting over himself and the truck floor.

There was little talking among us as we rode, but I heard snatches of conversation from a few of the stronger ones.

'We are lucky. We will get treatment.'

'Who is the man driving this truck?'

'I don't know. Maybe we will find out soon.'

'How far away could this hospital be?'

After what seemed like three hours, the truck finally stopped.

Outside I could see a small solitary building which appeared to be a hospital. Some Tanzanian nurses in white jackets arrived to carry us out of the truck. We were taken to a tent that had been erected beside the building. Inside were hospital beds with drips and other medical equipment.

I didn't fully understand where we were. Was this a Non-Governmental Organisation clinic or a simple village hospital that we had been taken to? I was too weak to ask anyone.

I was placed onto one of the beds and within minutes a nurse had inserted a drip into my arm. The other boys and young lady were also treated.

These drips seemed to be pouring life back into our veins.

Just an hour later, I began to feel better, more alert and a little stronger.

Another hour passed and a nurse arrived to remove the needle.

I'd imagined we'd be staying in the hospital until we had recovered, but I realised this was not the case.

I was handed a few boxes containing a drug called 'Negram', a tablet to cure dysentery, then the nurses came to lift me again.

They carried me outside to the waiting truck. We were being taken back to Heru-Ushingo that same day.

The white man, whose name I still didn't know, appeared, ready to drive us back. Within another three hours we had returned back to Heru-Ushingo. By then, night had fallen.

People crowded around the truck to help lift us out.

As Havyarimana was being carried, I heard several shocked exclamations.

'Oh, he is gone!'

'He didn't make it!'

'Havyarimana has died!'

Havyarimana's lifeless body was placed on the ground next to the truck.

It was true. Unbeknown to any of us who had been riding with him, Havyarimana had passed away during the journey back to Heru-Ushingo. We thought he had been sleeping, but instead he had been too weak to recover from his illness, despite the Negram and rehydration fluids he had just been given. They had come too late for him.

What a shock it was to hear this. And what a tragedy to witness, knowing he hadn't survived despite the amazing gift of treatment we had all been given.

That could have been any one of us, I thought. *How blessed we have been.*

I was helped to my feet and given support to stand up. The white man who had driven us was standing close by and I managed to say a quick 'thank you' to him. He smiled back at me and nodded his head. Then, as soon as the last student had left the truck, he climbed back inside and drove off again.

I never saw or heard of him again.

I never even learned who he was or why he had chosen to help us.

Everything felt so surreal.

Earlier that day, I had been on my deathbed, feeling my life drain away from me. But now, life had returned to me.

Lord, you saved me! Again! I cannot believe what you have done for me.

I didn't know who was responsible for choosing to take us to the hospital. But I couldn't believe it was sheer luck that such a random act of kindness had happened to me. Only five people had been taken that day. It appeared the driver had chosen students as he believed we would be the most useful to our fellow refugees if we survived.

I was convinced it was another amazing act of God that my life had been saved.

He seemed to be protecting me. But why? It was the one question I asked myself over and over again.

By the next morning, I felt so much better and had managed to sit up. The Negram helped me feel stronger with each dose. Mama's expression was full of joy as she watched me recover. I knew she had believed I was as good as dead.

A few weeks later, we celebrated another display of God's mercy when my father returned home to us. He had been gone for two months and had finally felt well enough to manage the five-hour walk home.

The hospital Papa had visited was very basic and had only provided him with enough rehydration fluids to sustain him. This meant he wasn't entirely cured. But the nurses had given me a large amount of Negram tablets so I had some left over to share with Papa. This eventually rid him of his dysentery. Having learned that two of my cousin's children who had been at the hospital with him had died, I knew his recovery was another favour God had granted.

He seemed to be with me and was answering my prayers in incredible ways. I was certain it was him.

But what was God doing and why?

Why had he moved to spare my life so many times?

For a second I dared to imagine God had a wonderful purpose for my life outside of the misery I seemed to be trapped in.

I would see many more years of hardship and witness many more shows of God's amazing power, before I would discover what this purpose would be.

8

A Ray of Hope

Not long after my father had recovered from dysentery, he made a decision that would have been viewed as insane – even suicidal – by many. He announced it to me as we sat outside his hut talking one afternoon.

'Theo, we cannot live like this any more,' he told me. 'We are going back to Burundi.'

'Back to Burundi? Are you sure?' I said. 'But when do you plan to go?'

'I will leave by myself in a few days,' Papa said. 'I will go to another piece of land I own and begin to cultivate it. When it is ready, I will come back and bring Mama and the kids with me. You can come with us if you wish.'

Others may not have understood, but Papa didn't need to explain his reasons to me. I knew what they were.

Yes, we had endured much and risked our lives many times over to escape the killings and civil war in Burundi. But to us refugees, we had removed ourselves only to fight against other enemies that were equally destructive: hunger and disease. Papa knew we had been fortunate to recover from dysentery, but each day we witnessed more and more bodies being brought out for burial. He believed it was only a matter of time before we would succumb to it again. And even if disease didn't claim us soon, our bodies were weakening from the effects of malnutrition and lack of food.

Father's plan was to recover a piece of land he had previously bought in another remote neighbourhood. It was a very poor Hutu neighbourhood and one which he thought the Army was unlikely to trouble. It would have been unsafe to return to their old community where Tutsi locals might be tempted to seek revenge for the killings that had happened there. Papa wanted to return to his Government job so that he could begin collecting his salary again. Then he would cultivate the new land to provide food for his family. This way, they would have enough to eat and would escape the plague of dysentery, too.

There was always information being brought to the border of Tanzania by Burundians who were still piling into the country as refugees. After Papa had gained enough information to ensure he could find a safe route back into the country, avoiding areas of recent trouble, he left Heru-Ushingo, just as he had planned.

It was a month before Papa returned again. His report was hopeful. He had recovered his land, built a hut, made some basic plantations of cassavas, beans, sweet potatoes and other root vegetables, and he had also returned to his job as an Agricultural Monitor.

The country was still in the grips of civil war. The Army continued to carry out executions of Hutus and localised violence still erupted as Hutu and Tutsi grudges were unleashed. Politically, however, there were efforts being made for the country's stability. Another Hutu President, Cyprien Ntaryamira, had been installed in February 1994 and many Hutus were hopeful order would be restored soon.

As for myself, I wasn't ready to return to Burundi yet. After everything I had witnessed and heard, the thought still filled me with fear.

Some of my student friends had found work on local plantations and I hoped to do the same. The money would help me buy food to eat. It would also buy me more time to figure out if I could improve my quality of life in Tanzania.

As we bid each other goodbye before their trek back to Burundi, my parents and siblings said little. I gave Mama a hug and affectionately patted the backs of my brothers and sisters. Hanging in the air around us was the unmentionable reality that this could be the last time we saw each other.

I couldn't be sure if my family were making a good decision. Who knew what might happen on their journey back? And if they arrived safely, would they be able to make a new start for themselves without living in fear for their lives every day? Who knew how long the war might last or if the situation would deteriorate? But these were risks they were willing to take.

I prayed again in my heart for their wellbeing.

Lord, keep my family safe. And please let us see each other again one day. Let us see each other again in peaceful times.

Trying to suppress my anxiousness after my family's departure, I turned my focus to finding work. I approached local plantations and told them I was willing to provide manual labour. Tanzanian farmers had started allowing refugees to help with jobs such as removing weeds or digging. The catch was that the wages were pitiful. But for us, it would buy the extra food we craved.

Along with my student friends, I found work on a cassava plantation, pulling out weeds. On our first shift, we were promised 300 Tanzanian shillings (about 10 pence) but, at the end of the day, the owner refused to pay us. He offered us cassavas to eat instead. Already feeling humiliated by the nature of the work we had to do, we felt even more dehumanised by his deception. After all, we were helpless to protest. Reluctantly, since we had little choice, we accepted the cassavas. We didn't have a bag to carry them back with us, so we plucked long strands of grass that we braided together to make a sheet and then used it to scoop the cassavas up.

Carrying home our vegetables, it was impossible not to feel angry and frustrated. Even our Tanzanian brothers did not value the hard labour we were forced to carry out for our survival. Even in our lowest state, they were happy to exploit us. Was there really no one who cared for us and our pitiful circumstances?

That same month, we had a new visitor to Heru-Ushingo. She represented something we had been hoping and praying to see, something we believed might never arrive.

Her name was Suzanna and she was from Switzerland. She worked for an NGO called *Médecins Sans Frontières* (MSF).

Wearing a white medical jacket, our fair-skinned visitor could have been a mirage. Her tall frame and loose brown hair, which flowed over her shoulders, caught everyone's attention. Suzanna arrived alone, driving a truck labelled with the letters 'MSF'. The refugees flocked to her side on her arrival, eager to discover the purpose of her visit. I joined the group crowding around her.

'I am from an organisation which is concerned about the Burundian refugees,' she told us after introducing herself in French, a language Burundians were taught in schools because of our colonial ties to Belgium. 'I have been sent to help your people and I am looking for some nurses to work with me,' she continued. 'Is anyone here a nurse?'

It had now been five months since I arrived in Tanzania. Suzanna's words were undoubtedly one of the best things I had heard. They showed us the world knew we were here and urgently needed help. The excitement that now rippled the crowd grew. Suzanna had been sent to help save our lives.

Three women stepped forward to say they were nurses and one asked, 'How much will you pay us?'

Suzanna frowned. 'Pay? I'm afraid we cannot pay you for this work.'

'No pay? Then I cannot work for you.'

'We need money!'

'Yes, we need money!'

'But I am coming to help your own people . . .' Suzanna said, taken aback by a reaction she hadn't expected. 'We need your help to do this.'

But the nurses shook their heads and dispersed back into the crowd.

I was amazed by the response to Suzanna's request. Suddenly, I found myself pushing my way forward through the crowd.

'I'll help you,' I said. 'I'll do anything I can. I want to help my people. My name is Theo.'

Suzanna's face seemed to relax as she extended her hand towards me.

'Pleased to meet you, Theo,' she said. 'Thank you so much! I really could use any help I can get.'

Since Suzanna could not speak Kirundi, she welcomed me as a translator and also as someone who could help her start treating the diseases that were claiming lives among the refugees.

'I will train you to help me as if you were a nurse,' Suzanna told me. 'You can begin by translating for me and then I will need you to show the people how to take their medicines and to help disinfect wounds, too. We'll work until 4 p.m. each day. Afterwards, I will train you to do more things.'

That day, I was the only person who volunteered to help Suzanna. Despite this setback, Suzanna put herself to work right away. She had brought a tent with her, which she set up among the settlements of the refugees. Then she brought out a small table and some boxes of medication from the truck, positioning them under the shade of a tree. She invited those who were ill, especially children, to come and see her. She had supplies of Negram and rehydration salts to treat those suffering with dysentery, as well as a water dispenser to provide clean water for those needing a clean rehydration source. Hundreds were drawn to speak to Suzanna and collect medicines from her. I helped her communicate with the Burundians who spoke only Kirundi, and gave out the medicines as she directed.

For the first time in a very long time, I felt significant. Here was a chance to really serve my people and help save lives. Was this why God had spared my own life so many times?

After our work was over for the day, Suzanna invited me to have dinner with her. She had a gas stove burner and tins of canned food which she used to make a simple meal of chicken and rice with hot tea. It was the most delicious thing I had eaten in a long while and the best payment she could have given me.

The following day, Suzanna set up her medical table again. This time, she had arranged for two Tanzanian nurses to join her. It would be another month until more Burundians like myself would volunteer.

Suzanna arranged for the dispensary to distribute her medical supplies as more and more people came forward to be treated. She taught me how to observe symptoms of conditions such as malaria, malnutrition and dehydration, as well as other illnesses, so I could hand out the appropriate treatments. In time, she also taught me about vaccinations and how to administer them. We vaccinated most of the Burundian children living in Heru-Ushingo against diseases such as polio, tuberculosis and measles. As more people came forward to volunteer, a nutrition centre was started. We would distribute ingredients to make a nutritious porridge and teach refugees how to recognise symptoms of illness and malnutrition in their children.

Suzanna was a kind and humble lady. Even though my clothes were stained and smelly, and I was tick-infested, just as the rest of the refugees were, Suzanna never once showed any aversion to having me around her. Instead she treated me with generosity and compassion, often sharing her meals with me. Eventually she managed to pay me 300 Tanzanian shillings per day, along with the other volunteers she had. It wasn't much, but it was a great help and it was a wonderful day when I managed to purchase a new set of clean clothes for myself after saving my salary.

Of course, to the rest of the refugees, Suzanna's arrival was like the sun emerging from behind the clouds. It was the first and biggest sign of hope being restored to our people. We didn't have to die of disease and starvation, forgotten and unnoticed. The world knew about our suffering and they really did care. Things were going to get better. Not long afterwards, more NGOs arrived to help us and things changed dramatically for us refugees. Could we dare to hope life would be better now? That we might have a better future? It wouldn't be long before we discovered the realities of our predicament as refugees of a civil war.

9

Mtabila

The arrival of *Médecins Sans Frontières* was just the start of a turn in our fortune. Soon after, we were given assistance by two other major NGOs, World Concern and Oxfam. World Concern brought us staples of food that promised to end the aching hunger in our stomachs. Supplies of maize, lentils, green peas, porridge mix, salt and cooking oil were handed out. They also provided cooking pots and utensils, water storage containers, plastic waterproof sheets for our shelters and extra clothing. Oxfam worked to ensure the refugees had access to clean, safe water. They transported tanks of water along with them and later pumped out water from the river into a purifier. MSF continued to monitor and treat the health issues that existed among the refugees. With all these efforts being made on our behalf, we began to hope again. Those diseases that had loomed over our head, threatening death just weeks before, were now being eradicated. And we had free food now, food that would sustain us and restore health to our bodies. One of my duties as a medical assistant for MSF included visiting families and showing them how to plant vegetables.

Perhaps another NGO might come soon and set up some schools for us students, I dreamed as I continued to witness the improvements around us. *Then I would have everything I need. I could work for MSF and continue my studies, too.*

A few weeks later came a report that was sickening to hear. Our new-found optimism was shattered. Some refugees who had brought radios along with them related another catastrophic event had happened in Burundi.

'The new President has been killed!'

'Cyprien Ntaryamira has died in a plane crash!'

'It was murder!'

'They destroyed our Hutu leader again!'

It was devastating news. On 6 April 1994, Ntaryamira had been travelling aboard a plane from Tanzania to Rwanda, along with the Rwandan President, Juvénal Habyarimana, a fellow Hutu. Their plane had been shot down in Rwanda by unknown assailants. This had also sparked off civil war and mass killings in Rwanda, particularly of Rwandan Tutsis by Rwandan Hutus. This was later known as the 1994 Rwandan Genocide.

As for Burundi, although the event was likely carried out by Rwandan perpetrators, the loss of our Hutu leader meant our Government would be in turmoil again, lacking the power to control the unrest that was already at large in the country. The Tutsi Army would have the freedom to murder as they desired.

I was anxious for the safety of my family. I had heard reports they were doing well after they returned, but now I feared their lives would be in danger again.

And what of Burundi? Would it ever see peace?

My heart was full of pain for my country. Was it destined to be in turmoil forever?

I wondered if I would ever return to my homeland.

Not long after Ntaryamira's death, we received major news about our displacement. More than six months after the

Burundian war had started, the United Nations High Commissioner of Refugees (UNHCR) was setting up a formal refugee camp 30 miles away from Heru-Ushingo. Named 'Mtabila', it would give Burundian refugees a place to be received and cared for. The camp would ensure we had food to eat every day and healthcare, too. There was even a plan to set up a primary school. Beyond that we didn't expect much more, but, at the time, the new camp sounded like a magnificent haven compared to our current living conditions.

Big trucks arranged by the UN arrived in Heru-Ushingo to transport us all to the new camp, a piece of barren land which I estimated stretched over 40 square miles. There were no boundaries set in place yet, as the location had been chosen to house up to 200,000 refugees and was set to expand as demand required. We brought with us what little belongings we had. For me, it was just an extra set of clothing in a cloth bag. We were required to register on arrival and would then be allocated a plot of land situated on our new campsite. We would also be given the materials to build our own waterproof shelters.

It was during my move there that another act of providence brought me into the path of two good friends from my past. They were brothers I had known from my school days, Jean Baptist Muzima, who we called 'Muzima', and his younger brother Thierry Bahizi. Muzima was one of my mentors from the Christian Union I had been part of. He had taught me how to read and interpret the Bible. His brother Thierry had been in the year below me at school. The two brothers had only just arrived in Tanzania from Burundi where they had been in hiding since the death of President Ndadaye. I was overjoyed to have found them and even happier when they invited me to share the shelter they had been constructing for themselves on their allocated plot. They were erecting four shelters to share among ten boys. They were Christians and I was grateful to have found these friends to live with.

The shelters were very basic. We used branches, twine made from tree fibres and blades of grass to build the walls and roofs. We were given plastic sheets to place on the roofs to make the shelters waterproof. After attaching these sheets over our heads, we covered them with additional layers of branches and grass. Our beds were also made by securing a mass of branches together with twine. We heaped bunches of grass on top of them for our mattresses and topped them with one of the plastic sheets we had been given. I was invited to share a room with Thierry in the biggest shelter being made. It had four rooms. Three were used as bedrooms and one as a communal area. Muzima was also in the same shelter, along with three boys I hadn't met before, Eliphaz, Marc and Felix.

We took it in turns to cook our rationed food outside in the pots we had also been given. Another task we shared was looking for firewood. This was one thing the UNHCR did not provide us with. Initially, since we were in a forest, this would not prove a problem.

Of all the boys, Thierry became my closest ally. Thierry was a popular young man because he was talkative and good at telling stories. He had a face that was constantly animated. I also liked him because he was smart and bold. Out of everyone, I felt I could confide in Thierry the most. During our time living together, we would often share our feelings about the war and our country, Burundi. Like me, Thierry also harboured a strong desire to study again. We would talk about our hopes of continuing our education. We daydreamed together. Perhaps the war would end soon and peace would come. Then we could return to Burundi and our studies.

Now that we had been relocated to the refugee camp, we were no longer struggling for survival. This gave us time to think about something we had previously been unsure would exist for us – the future. Having joined these Christian brothers, prayer and seeking God became an important ritual we shared. We conducted daily prayer between 5 and 6 p.m. each day and, every Friday, we held overnight prayer meetings where we would stay up the whole night to pray and cry out to God. We even built a fifth shelter on our plot where we would meet to conduct these prayer meetings, joined by other Christian students we had met in the camp. At its height, there were about twenty of us.

We sang songs of worship and also composed our own songs to God that were inspired by David's lamenting psalms, seeking answers to how long our suffering and displacement would carry on. We asked God when he would finally answer the desires of our hearts that we lifted up to him in prayer. We held many in common: we were anxious for our families to remain safe, desperate for the war to end and to return to our country, and longing for a peaceful and contented future. Another hope we all shared was that we would be in heaven one day. We looked forward to that time, believing the world was too unkind and sour for us.

During the day, I worked as a Nursing Assistant in the camp's hospital tent, attending to the sick and distributing appropriate medicines. The role was rewarding as it gave me a purpose. But when my work was completed, my heart burned with a desire to seek God and cry out to him in prayer. I believed I had a living and powerful God. He had shown me just how powerful he was when he had spared my life numerous times. I was still desperate to know the reason why. Surely God had a great plan and a future for me outside of the camp? But how could

Theo and Thierry in Mtabila, after purchasing new clothes. Photo taken before their escape to Kenya.

Theo and Thierry ready for their Sunday ministry to refugees in Nairobi, 1997.

Theo leading worship at the Burundian and
Rwandese refugees service at Calvary Worship
Centre in Nairobi, 1998.

Theo (holding the guitar), Thierry (far left),
Gervais (far right) and other students during their time
at Carlile College.

Thierry (left) and Theo (centre) graduating from
Carlile College, summer 2000.

Theo going to train church leaders in the
Mtabila camp, 2004.

Theo, Christine and his four children, Précise, Prévoyant, Kerry Princia and Danny Prince.

Theo and Hezroni Ntizompeba in August 2017. Theo and Hezroni's ministries continue to work closely together.

that be when there was no certainty the tensions in Burundi would ever improve? Besides, what was possible for me now that I could no longer study?

It was hard to resist my old anger and bitterness returning. So history had repeated itself. Just like Papa, I had been robbed of my chance to educate myself and do something great with my life. My biggest dream had been wrenched from me. Our Tutsi enemies had slaughtered so many of my Hutu brothers and sisters and, of those of us who were left, mostly contained within the walls of refugee camps, we lacked the means to prosper and create a future for ourselves. Such thoughts always enraged me, even enough to make me wish I could go back to Burundi and fight with the Hutu rebels who were resisting the Army. Then I could avenge my brothers for all the suffering we had had to endure, for the family and friends we had seen massacred, for the homes that had been ransacked and burned, and for the inhumane conditions we had endured because we could no longer live on our own soil. The troubling thing was, whenever my spirit felt that familiar swell of hatred, my thoughts would always go back to that incident with Godance, when she had thrown her arms around my neck and offered her Tutsi life to protect my Hutu one. Then I would feel ashamed of my feelings. I was sure God had used her on purpose to remind me that I shouldn't be so hateful.

As I sought God more and more, I felt these convictions grow stronger. God was stirring something in my heart. Something I hadn't been expecting at all.

One day, after having been at the camp for over nine months, and while reading a Bible I had managed to obtain, I was struck by a passage I was studying on the crucifixion of Jesus:

When they came to the place called the Skull, they crucified him there, along with the criminals – one on his right, the other on his left. Jesus said, 'Father, forgive them, for they do not know what they are doing.' And they divided up his clothes by casting lots.

Luke 23:33,34

The words seemed to jump out at me and my skin pricked with goose bumps. Here was Jesus, a man so good and innocent of any wrongdoing, having his life taken away from him as if he was a foul criminal. But even as they crucified him, right during the very act, Jesus was able to forgive those who were killing him and asked that his heavenly Father did the same. This realisation convicted me deeply. Wasn't this the same forgiveness God expected from me? If Jesus could forgive those who were killing him, even in the very act of their murder, wasn't I expected to forgive those who I felt were persecuting me and my people?

But how could I bring myself to do that?

That night, I tossed and turned on my grass mattress. For some reason I couldn't get those words from the Bible out of my head.

But even more disturbing to me, my mind kept returning to another incident that had happened months back as I had fled Burundi. I remembered the chicken I had caught and killed to eat from our Tutsi neighbour, Ngezahayo's yard. A new conviction dawned on me – I had been wrong to take Ngezahayo's chicken. Yes, my neighbour had already been killed by Hutus and his only surviving family member, his daughter-in-law, Jeane, had fled their home. But I felt that more than the act of theft, God was convicting me about my motives in taking that chicken. For I had taken it with malice in my heart, feeling a vicious hatred towards my Tutsi neighbour because of the devastation of my village which I blamed him and all Tutsis for.

Now I sensed God telling me he was unhappy with how I had felt and acted.

Then came an even more disturbing revelation.

God didn't just want me to feel sorry about my actions, he wanted me to make amends for them.

An instruction came to me that I was sure was not of my own will or creation. There was no way it could have been as it was something that even to my own thoughts sounded absurd: '*Go back to Burundi and ask forgiveness for the chicken that you stole.*'

Lord, I said, *is that you speaking this thought? Is that something you really want me to do? Surely not, Lord! You wouldn't want me to risk my life to go back to say sorry. Not just for a chicken I took.*

But no matter how much I tried to shake the instruction or convince myself I was imagining things, the words would spring back into my mind.

Go back to Burundi and ask forgiveness for the chicken that you stole!

That night, I could barely sleep. As hard as I tried, the turmoil in my spirit wouldn't cease. By the next morning I was exhausted. I felt very sorry for having taken Ngezahayo's chicken in spite. I wished I hadn't done it now.

Lord, forgive me, I prayed. *You have convicted me that I was wrong in my thoughts and actions.*

But those words kept haunting me.

Go back to Burundi and ask forgiveness for the chicken that you stole!

Though I knew God would forgive me, was God telling me that I needed to gain forgiveness from Ngezahayo's family, too?

But how could I do that? Ngezahayo and most of his family had died. Only his daughter-in-law, Jeane, had escaped unhurt.

You know where she lives! Go and find her and ask for her forgiveness!

Was I going crazy? Surely it was my own mind making up these orders. God wouldn't want me to go back to Burundi and apologise for a chicken I stole.

If I had been able to convince myself I was being ridiculous or that my mind was just playing tricks on me, I would have happily pushed aside such thoughts.

But the truth was, that day, my conviction of what I needed to do only grew stronger and more urgent.

God was a good and gracious God, but I knew I had acted wrongly. And however slight I might have thought my actions were in comparison to all the other hateful acts the war had spewed, I knew my deed had still offended him.

The words that Jesus spoke in Matthew 5:21,22, revisited me:

> You have heard that it was said to the people long ago, 'You shall
> not murder, and anyone who murders will be subject to judg-
> ment.' But I tell you that anyone who is angry with a brother
> or sister will be subject to judgment. Again, anyone who says to
> a brother or sister, 'Raca', [an Aramaic term of contempt] is an-
> swerable to the court. And anyone who says, 'You fool!' will be in
> danger of the fire of hell.

The God I knew was a Holy God and my sin was ugly to him. I knew I wouldn't be able to rest until I had made amends in the way I felt God was asking me to. Weeks earlier, while we were still in Heru-Ushingo, I had heard some news about Ngezahayo's daughter-in-law from a villager I knew. He had just arrived as a refugee and had passed her home just 12 miles from the border. She was still living in Ruhinga, the same village I was from, having remarried another neighbour of ours, Pierre, who had also lost his spouse in the war. Now I realised it couldn't have been a coincidence that this information about her location had been brought to me.

God really must want me to go back to Burundi and make amends for the sin I committed!

Choosing to tell no one about my plan (surely they would label me insane?), I made a decision. It was one that filled me with fear and every fibre of my rational mind was resisting, but I knew I had to be obedient to what I felt God was telling me. After all, I needed to feel his peace again. How could I continue my existence with the knowledge that God had been grieved by me? I needed to know he would continue to be with me and bless me during the difficult times I had been enduring.

And so, I prepared myself for what lay ahead.

The following night, I was going to make my way back to Burundi.

10

Making Amends

With a feeling of dread in the pit of my stomach, I planned my exit from the camp and from Tanzania. I would begin my journey during the early morning hours so there was less chance of being seen. Since being transferred to an official United Nations camp, one of the difficulties every refugee faced was the new laws we were bound by. This included needing permission from the Camp Commander if we ever wanted to leave it. But gaining this permission wasn't easy. We would need to show some kind of proof that we had a valid reason and destination, such as needing medical aid or having to visit a friend or relative who might have ended up in a Tanzanian prison. Often a bribe would change hands, too. And the repercussions for being caught were extremely severe. Violators would be sent to a Tanzanian prison for six months and then returned to Burundi.

I had heard there was a path out of the camp through the surrounding forest that would enable me to leave without being seen by the armed Tanzanian police officers who patrolled its perimeters. The day before I planned to leave, I talked to a few refugees who were involved in smuggling goods into the camp. They gave me information about the best way to leave the camp without attracting attention.

As much as I tried, I couldn't quash the fear that seemed to flood every part of my body. What would happen if I was caught leaving the camp? Or what if I made it to Burundi and ran into a Tutsi mob again? Was I set to die in my attempt to apologise over a stolen chicken?

I battled with the possibilities that kept popping up in my mind over what might await me on my journey. But then came a stronger conviction. Surely it was God who wanted me to return to Burundi? If that were the case, I would have to trust he would keep me safe. I had seen him protect my life so many times already. Now I needed to believe he would do it again. And if my life was lost in the process of my journey, at least I would be able to meet God with a clear conscience.

I left our shelter at 5 a.m., too afraid to leave when it was dark. The boys in my shelter were all asleep and I had managed to keep my flight a secret from them. I carried nothing with me except the money I had saved from my salary as a Nursing Assistant. The notes were stuffed in my pocket and I intended to use them as compensation for the chicken I had taken.

Following a safe route through the forest I had been told about, I left the camp without being detected and headed towards the Tanzanian border.

I spent the majority of the day travelling towards Heru-Ushingo. Arriving in the afternoon, I spent the night there. The next day, I rose early again and headed towards the River Malagarasi. The point I arrived at had two commercial boats operating river crossings at its bank. Their routes also brought their passengers to a landing point in Burundi where there was no swampland.

Arriving on Burundian soil again, I felt a mixture of relief and fear. This was the country I loved and craved to return to. But it was also a place where my life was in danger.

In particular, there was one area I had to pass which I had been dreading since I had begun my journey. It was a sugar cane factory which stood three miles away from the trunk road the ferry boat had brought us to. Across from it, an Army camp had been erected. The area would be swarming with soldiers and I would have to pass them without drawing attention to myself. I knew my survival depended on blending in as a poor Hutu, trying to go about my daily business. If someone sensed I was a student trying to return to the country, I could be stopped and questioned . . . or worse.

As I approached the sugar cane factory, I was sure my heart was pounding so wildly someone was bound to notice. There were dozens of soldiers in the area. Many wore uniforms and carried Kalashnikov rifles as they circulated around or stood in groups, talking. There were also a handful of other poor labourers walking past the sugar cane factory. I knew it was important to blend in with them.

I kept my head down and my shoulders hunched. I was hopeful this would add to my already unkempt appearance and convince any curious Army soldiers that I was just another poor farmer travelling along the route.

Let me be invisible, God, I prayed. *Don't let anyone see me.*

Perspiration prickled my face and I could feel myself trembling as I continued to walk by.

Would the soldiers pick up on my fear? Would they notice I wasn't one of the locals? What would I say to them if they questioned me?

My trembling legs continued to carry me along.

I held my breath, waiting for a voice to call to me or for a hand to reach out to stop my progress.

My heart kept up its furious rhythm in my chest.

Any second now, they might see me . . . Any second now, they might spot I'm not a local.

To my amazement, I was left untroubled. I passed by without anyone saying a word.

As each of my steps took me further away from the factory and the Army camp, my nerves finally began to settle.

I had avoided detection. God had protected me!

Thank you, Lord!

I couldn't help feeling more confident that the journey I was making was part of God's will for me and that he would be with me to make it a success.

Lord, I am believing in your protection! Please don't abandon me. Help me with what lies ahead.

I was still uncertain and anxious about what would greet me as I continued my journey, but I knew I had to stick to the plan I had made. I needed to reach the village of Ruhinga and find Jeane as soon as I could.

It took me more than five hours of walking to finally reach Ruhinga. I spotted a couple of cowherds bringing in the cows from the fields, a sign the sun would be setting soon.

It was easy to find our old neighbour Pierre's house, a small square hut made of mud and dry woven leaves. I walked up to its wooden door and knocked gently on it. Jeane's surprised, then confused, expression greeted me as she discovered me in her doorway.

'Theo? What are you doing here? Are you okay?'

For a second I almost couldn't get my words out.

'Er . . . hello, Jeane . . . I am well. I . . . I . . . just came to see you and speak to you.'

'You did?' Jeane replied. 'Okay, then please do come in.'

'Oh no . . . I can't stay,' I said. 'I just came here to ask you something.'

Jeane raised her eyebrows.

How would she react to what I was about to say?

'You see . . . about nine months ago, when I returned to our neighbourhood, I saw so many had been killed or had run away and I was so sad to see everything that had happened. I was also hungry so I did something I now regret . . . I stole a chicken from your father-in-law's house . . .'

I paused to wait for Jeane's response.

She didn't say a word but nodded at me to continue.

'The . . . the truth was, I could have taken a chicken from my own yard, but I was angry about the war and with your family for being Tutsis . . . So I took Ngezahayo's chicken and killed it out of spite for everything that had happened in our village. But now God has convicted me I was wrong in doing this and I'd like to make amends. Since Ngezahayo is no more, I brought some money with me to give to you for the chicken I took. I hope you can forgive me for what I did . . .'

Now Jeane's eyes narrowed and she seemed to glare at me. I couldn't read her expression. Was she furious about my confession? Hurt? Shocked? I couldn't tell.

Finally, she spoke.

'Theo, was it just one chicken you took? Is that why you came here?'

'Er . . . yes, Jeane,' I said.

'The war made us lose so much,' she said. 'Chickens . . . cows . . . our home . . . the lives of my family. There were so many other things that were taken from us . . . but have you really come to see me about one chicken?'

'Yes, Jeane,' I said. 'I only took one chicken. But it was wrong of me and I want to make amends.'

I brought out my Tanzanian notes from my pocket.

'Please accept some money as compensation for it, as well as my apology.'

Jeane raised her hand in protest.

'Oh no, Theo!' she said, shaking her head. 'Oh no! I'm sorry but I am not going to take anything from you.'

My heart sank.

'You won't,' I said. 'But why not? It's important that I make amends. I really am sorry.'

Jeane looked me straight in the eyes. I noticed her own filling up with tears.

Then she said something that took me by complete surprise. After making my apology, it was the last thing I had expected to hear.

'Theo, I won't take your money and I won't hold a grudge,' she said. 'But now that you have asked for my forgiveness, I want you to do something else in return for it . . . forgive me and my family, too! We were the ones who stole the iron sheets from the roof of your father's house after he left.'

I was amazed by what I was hearing. Here I was, having travelled for two days, and risking my life, to ask forgiveness from a Tutsi. But now Jeane was asking for my forgiveness, too.

I was struck by a profound understanding of what was taking place.

That evening, I believed God had set me up to be part of a wonderful exchange of repentance and forgiveness. He was teaching me a lesson I needed to learn – that just as my people had been wronged, we too had wronged others. I also learned first-hand, as the Bible taught, that we couldn't ask to be forgiven if we ourselves weren't willing to forgive those who had hurt us. God had used Jeane to teach me a beautiful truth about the power of forgiveness.

I could tell Jeane's apology was genuine. She, too, carried guilt about her theft from my father's home. Here we were, guilty of the same crime, and she needed my forgiveness as much as I needed hers.

'Of course, Jeane,' I replied. I couldn't control the smile on my face. 'Of course I will accept your apology for what was taken. Just as you have accepted mine.'

Jeane smiled now. 'Thank you, Theo,' she said. 'I am so happy to hear that. Now, please do come inside.'

It was growing dark and I was eager to travel another couple of miles more that night to visit my parents.

'I must leave now,' I told her. 'It won't be safe for me to travel if I don't. But thank you for your graciousness. It means so much to me.'

I bid Jeane goodbye and turned from her doorstep.

A huge weight had been lifted from me. I had done what I had set out to do. The Lord had allowed me to make amends for my offence and now my burden was gone. Peace had been restored to my previously troubled spirit and I knew I could return to Mtabila with a contented heart. Before I did, I needed to see how my parents and siblings were doing.

That night I continued walking to Nyembuye, the new village where they had set up home. Arriving at their newly constructed shack, Mama and Papa were truly excited to see me again. I was equally overjoyed and relieved to see my family was well. Mama was heavily pregnant, expecting her eighth child, and Papa was growing enough food to feed everyone while continuing to work as an Agricultural Monitor. So far, they had not sensed any threat towards them after returning to Burundi. They lived in a very quiet village and no one had come to trouble them. I also learned that my grandfather lived in a small shelter close to my parents. My grandmother and grandfather had survived the day the Army had attacked their village, but sadly my grandmother had passed away months later after falling ill.

I felt tempted to stay in Burundi with my parents, but we were all aware that Hutu students were still being targeted by the Army and angry Tutsis. There was still no hope of me being able to study so it was best I returned to Tanzania. After spending a couple of days with my parents, I borrowed a bicycle from my brother and rode back across the Tanzanian border and then on to Mtabila. Once again, God protected me on my way. I faced no trouble on the long and tiring journey.

Back at the camp, Thierry quizzed me about my absence.

'Where did you go Theo?' he said. 'You didn't tell us. We were worried!'

How could I have explained the wonderful lesson God had used to change my heart and teach me about my need to forgive my Tutsi brothers and sisters . . . and about my own need to be forgiven, too? Even then, I still couldn't see a bigger picture and how this lesson would have a lasting impact on my life and influence the course of my future.

'I just went to see my parents, Thierry,' I said. 'But there is no need to worry now. I am here again.'

And so this matter with Ngezahayo's chicken remained between God and me. Of course, God wasn't finished with the lessons he wanted to teach me. In the months to come, there would be many more to learn about my heavenly Father – who was also a mighty, faithful and loving God.

11

Bushman

Life in Mtabila continued and each day seemed to blend into the next without much difference. After visiting my parents in Burundi, my decision to return to the Tanzania UN camp was down to the belief my life would be in danger if I tried to continue my education during the civil war. Now wasn't the right time, I knew. But I still prayed that God would bring peace to Burundi so I could eventually go home.

I was confident I had the strength of mind and patience to wait out my time in Mtabila until then. I still held the conviction that God had a better plan for me, that he didn't want me to remain a destitute and helpless refugee forever.

In the meantime, I would be content with my work as a Nursing Assistant. It afforded me a sense of worth knowing I was able to help my people in such a way. With this small notion of purpose and my hope for a greater purpose intact, I felt that life in Mtabila was bearable for the time being.

But my feelings were about to drastically change.

My resolve to stay in the camp was suddenly shattered one day in an unexpected way.

It happened one afternoon, just a month after my trip to see Jeane, when I needed to make a journey to a Tanzanian store. Having saved my wages and being in need of some new clothes, I approached a young Westerner who worked for Oxfam. I didn't know him personally but, every day, I had watched him arrive by car to work in the camp. I also knew that all of the aid workers were living in Kasulu, the nearest town to the camp and the closest place to get the clothes I needed.

'Will you take me with you to Kasulu?' I asked the man. 'My clothes are worn and I would be grateful to buy some new ones.'

'Sure!' he told me, without much thought. 'It's no problem at all.'

We walked towards his car and I spotted his driver, a Tanzanian, leaning against it. As we approached, I noticed his driver's face twist in disgust.

I wondered what he was disturbed about, but before I could guess, the driver made his feelings clear in broken English.

'This man is coming with us?' he asked his employer, while glaring at me.

'Yes, why? What is the matter?'

'Drive your car if you want,' the driver told him. He threw the car keys to the man. 'I cannot sit inside it with a *Mshamba*!'

Then he walked off.

I was stunned.

A Mshamba! He had called me a Mshamba!

The Swahili word translated as 'man from the bush'.

To Tanzanians and Burundians, the term 'bushman' was a description for someone who was uncivilised and not regarded as a human being.

Had the Tanzanian driver really been so disgusted by me? Did he really despise the idea of being in the same car as me?

I couldn't believe another human being had found me so contemptible.

I was an impoverished refugee and lacked the money to keep up my appearance as I once had. Didn't the Tanzanians understand what we had been through or the pathetic living conditions we had no choice but to accept for our survival?

My Oxfam friend frowned and shook his head as he watched his driver walk away. I expected he would offer to drive us instead. But now his words caught me by surprise, too. He had been unnerved by his driver's reaction and was now scared about being alone with me.

'Perhaps it's best if I go by myself,' he told me. 'I'm sorry.'

I looked on helplessly as he got inside his car, started the engine and pulled away from the camp in a cloud of dust. I felt like I had just been punched in the stomach.

I was humiliated and had never felt so worthless in my entire life.

Even the Westerner had been swayed by the Tanzanian's opinion of me.

During my time as a refugee in Tanzania, I had lost everything, including any opportunities to better myself and my situation. This meant the only real thing I felt I had left was my sense of identity and worth.

Now even this had been dealt a blow I felt I couldn't recover from.

I had always believed my life had a purpose and that it was valuable, and I had clung onto these beliefs during my time in Tanzania. When the UN and other aid agencies had arrived, it had helped reinforce these convictions in my self-worth. Yes, the world knew my life and those of my countrymen were valuable, too. Yet what had happened that day with the Tanzanian and Westerner had given me an unpleasant dose of reality I could not stomach. The compassion I had hoped to find from strangers who might understand our plight had instead been replaced by contempt and repulsion. It tore down the only valuable possession I had been clinging to with all of my might.

I am really worthless to everyone, the Westerners and the Tanzanians! I thought. *They don't even consider me a human being like themselves. I am just a stench to their nostrils, that is all.*

The hurt I felt was agonising

But my initial feelings of self-pity weren't to last.

That's it! I thought. *I won't bear this any longer!*

A wave of anger replaced my pain.

I just couldn't bring myself to accept the insult that had been thrown in my face. I was not a worthless 'bushman' who deserved to be treated that way. I was an intelligent, civilised Burundian who had done nothing to deserve a title which described me as someone to be loathed and feared.

If this was how I was to be regarded in Tanzania by its citizens, who would view me with as much hatred as some Tutsis had for us, I decided I was no better off here than I was in my own country. I would never allow anyone to treat me that way again.

It might have been different if I had been able to study in Tanzania, but the reality was I couldn't. My prospects in Tanzania still remained hopeless and with opinions about Burundian refugees becoming increasingly unfavourable, I didn't see the point in staying any longer.

And so, with my feelings of frustration boiling over, I made a decision there would be no turning back from.

I was going to return home to Burundi. This time for good.

So strong were my feelings of hurt and humiliation that I didn't even stop to consider the consequences of my choice as I made my way back to my shelter. Instead, I placed what little clothes I owned into a cloth bag and resolved to leave first thing the next morning. I didn't want to spend another night in the camp. I wanted to go back to Burundi as soon as I could.

I informed the boys I lived with that this was my intention. Thierry was sad, but he understood how I felt. 'You will be missed,' he told me. 'But just go if you need to. There is nothing here anyway.'

Leaving the camp without permission, I followed the same forest route I had previously taken. Once again, I risked being caught and thrown into a Tanzanian jail. This time, however, I realised the fear and anxiousness I had carried with me during my last escape had completely vanished. Now I possessed only a deep pain, my anger and a solid determination. Even if I had to die in Burundi, at least I would die with my dignity. If other Hutus could remain in the country while the civil war continued, I could too. It would be worth the risk to escape the degrading circumstances I could no longer accept.

I travelled on to Heru-Ushingo, stayed one night, and made the ferry crossing over the River Malagarasi the following day, just as I had done previously. I arrived back at the point where I needed to pass the sugar cane factory and Army camp.

It was still dangerous to be recognised as a Hutu student, but now my former terror at being caught had left me. This time I walked past the factory and groups of Army soldiers as if I didn't have a care in the world. With my head up and my gaze fixed firmly in front of me, all I could think about was the humiliation I had suffered in Tanzania, about how I had been perceived as the lowest form of being that could exist. I was just too angry to think about what could happen to me if I was stopped. And in reality, I knew I didn't care any longer. I just wanted to be as far away from the refugee camp and my life there as I could. I was ready to accept whatever fate might throw at me as a result.

It must have been another act of God's protection that I was able to pass the Army camp again without being noticed.

I kept on walking and managed to reach my parents' village before sunset that afternoon.

'Theo, it is you!' my mother cried in surprise when I walked through the door of their shack. 'You are back again? But why?'

I didn't want to tell Mama the truth.

'I just wanted to see how things were here,' I told her. 'I needed to make sure you were all okay.'

Mama smiled, comforted to see that I was well. 'We are all fine,' she said. 'I am happy you are here. Come, meet your new baby sister and then let me get you something to eat.' The newest arrival to our family, Joyce, had been born a few weeks ago and it was wonderful to meet and hold her.

Afterwards, I sat outside the shack with Mama as she prepared a meal for me on the fire. I may not have known what the future held for me now, but it felt so good to be back home. We chatted and she filled me in on what had been happening in Burundi. A new Hutu President had been installed after President Ntaryamira's assassination but the Army was still revolting against the Government. Many schools were still closed and none of my siblings had resumed their education. Instead, they turned their hand to farming alongside Papa and Mama. Father was doing well, however. He was still working and Mama told me she expected him home any minute.

Before long, Mama was dishing up my food, but I noticed she seemed a little quiet.

'What's the matter, Mama?' I asked. 'Are you not feeling well?'

'No, I am fine Theo,' she said. 'It's just that it's getting late now. I wonder why your papa is not home yet.'

It was true, the sun had set and Papa was now a few hours late. It was unusual for him to be delayed.

Just then, I looked up and spotted a figure approaching the shack.

'Look, this must be him now,' I said. 'See, Mama . . .'

But the man who stepped inside our doorway wasn't my papa.

Instead it was my Uncle Nicodeme, the husband of my mum's cousin. He was also employed by the Ministry of Agriculture and worked alongside my father.

As Nicodeme stepped into the light of the shack, his expression revealed something was wrong.

His words tumbled out of his mouth before my head could make sense of them. And after it had, I was filled with alarm.

He said: 'It's your father. They've taken him. He's been arrested by the Army.'

12

Papa

Nicodeme trembled as he slumped down onto a stool to explain what had happened. He and Papa had been at a meeting when some Army soldiers had interrupted it and asked to speak to my father. They had taken him away in a car to the Gendarmerie, the paramilitary barracks, wanting to question him regarding some accusations made against him. At the same time, Nicodeme had seen them taking Papa's bicycle into custody along with him. This was the normal practice for people who were being arrested and that's when Nicodeme realised Papa was in trouble. He had raced home as soon as he could to tell Mama.

Though the soldiers had said nothing about the charge being brought against Papa, we were sure he was being accused of the murders of Tutsis in the war. We also knew my father was innocent, not least because he had been one of the first to escape to Tanzania after President Ndadaye's death. If I had lived in peaceful times, I would have been confident that Papa would soon be released, that our judicial system would discover his innocence. But these weren't normal times. Many prominent Hutu figures from all over the country were 'disappearing' without much explanation. My father had always been respected in his community and was active in the political realm. He had helped gather support for President Ndadaye in the 1993 elections. I wouldn't have been surprised if Tutsis from his old neighbourhood, finding out about his return to Burundi, had made false accusations against him in a bid to do him harm. As Mama and I listened to Nicodeme's report, I knew we were all thinking the same thing. Given a chance, the Army would kill Papa.

I had to do something to stop this from happening. I had to intervene before it was too late. But how?

My cousin Frédéric lived in a hut just 15 metres away from my parents' home. I saw him standing outside and went over to tell him the news about Papa. He had a close relationship with my father and I knew he would be saddened, too.

As I explained what Nicodeme had told us, Frédéric was determined to help.

'This is a very bad situation,' he said. 'They will kill him for sure. What can we do?'

Before I could formulate any useful thoughts, Frédéric grabbed my arm.

'I know a solution! We will see my old teacher,' he said. 'Come! We can't waste time.'

'Where are we going?' I asked, as he pulled me along.

As we hurried away, Frédéric managed to explain his plan.

A former Hutu teacher of his had become the Deputy Governor of the Province of Rutana, where my parents lived. If there was any chance we could contact him, the Deputy Governor could go to the Gendarmerie where Papa was and ensure nothing happened to him.

Now a five-hour walk to Rutana, the provincial capital, lay ahead of us. We chose a less-travelled route to get us there and had to spend the night sleeping in a forest so no one would see us. The plan was to reach the Deputy Governor's house as soon as morning broke. This way we wouldn't be wasting any time in getting Papa the help he needed. The Deputy Governor had been a good teacher to Frédéric and had been very fond of his pupils. However, neither of us could be certain he would act on behalf of my father. Even if he did, would he be able to stop him from being harmed?

It was six o'clock and the sun had just risen when we arrived at the door of the Deputy Governor's house. We knocked vigorously for a few minutes before a tall, portly man opened the door to us. His face betrayed we had just woken him up, but his expression perked up when he recognised Frédéric.

'What are you doing here?' he asked. 'Is everything okay, Frédéric?'

'Hello, sir,' Frédéric began. 'Excuse us for troubling you so early. This is my cousin, Theo. His father has just been arrested by the Army. But he is an innocent man. We are afraid he will be killed soon. We had hoped there is something you can do.'

The Deputy Governor scrutinised me with his sleep-heavy eyes.

I realised I was holding my breath.

Was he going to send us away?

'Come inside, boys,' he said slowly, beckoning us through the door. 'Let's talk . . .'

We sat down in his front room and Frédéric explained what had happened to my father and why we believed he had been arrested.

'If there is anything you can do,' I added, 'my family and I would be forever indebted. I know my father has done no wrong.'

The Deputy Governor appeared to be thinking for a moment. When he finally spoke, I was surprised by the confidence in his tone.

'Yes, I will help you,' he said. 'I am going to make sure your father is not hurt. Let me get dressed and we will go at once.'

I felt encouraged by his willingness to help. I hoped there was a well-founded reason for his confidence.

Lord, I prayed, *you must let him help Papa. Don't let the Army take Papa's life.*

How ironic that the very night I returned to Burundi, I had arrived to find my family in danger. Even so, I thanked God that I was there. If Mama had been by herself, she wouldn't have known what to do. At least now there was a chance we might save Papa.

The Deputy Governor was ready within minutes and he led us outside to his car.

'I'll find someone to get you to your home first,' he said. 'You need to bring some food for your father. I'll go straight to the Gendarmerie and will meet you there.'

Less than an hour later, we were dropped off close to my family's shack.

It was upsetting to see Mama so worried. I reassured her everything would be okay now that we had the Deputy Governor's help but, in truth, I still wasn't sure this would be the case.

I told Mama to make some food. She packed a meal of sweet potatoes and beans into a metal container.

Then we headed to the Gendarmerie.

Frédéric and I arrived there just before midday and I was revisited by the sickening feeling of dread. Would Papa be there when I arrived? Was he okay? Would I be allowed to see him?

As Frédéric waited outside, I approached the front desk of the station and gave the officer my father's name.

'I have some food to give him,' I said.

The officer pointed to a closed door, along a corridor.

'He is being questioned just now,' he said. 'Wait here and you can go inside after they are finished with him.'

After what seemed like a long wait, the door to the interrogation room opened and an Army officer walked out. The officer at the front desk beckoned to me so he could escort me to the room.

Papa was sitting inside, beside a long desk. He had his head in his hands and looked exhausted. When he glanced up and saw me, relief flooded his eyes.

I hoped Papa could see my relief, too. Now he knew we had seen he was well and that we would be sending him food, too. Burundian prisoners were always fed by family or friends, or they would have to go hungry. I took the food container and put it on the table next to him.

I managed to say a few words to Papa before I was ushered out again.

'Are you okay? Why have they arrested you?'

'They are saying I have murdered many Tutsis,' he told me. 'It is all lies.'

'That's enough talking,' the officer said sharply. He ushered me out and closed the door to the room behind us.

I returned to a seat near the front desk and sat down. I hung my head in my hands, too. An unbearable sense of anxiety filled me.

There was no way my father was a murderer. I knew he wasn't guilty of harming anyone. Someone must have brought a false accusation against him. But murder cases were notorious for being stretched out over years before anything even came to trial. Papa was likely to face a long spell in prison until a sentence was reached.

I felt completely helpless.

Lord! I cried out in my heart. *Why couldn't you have helped him? Where are you in the midst of all this trouble?*

In reality, if I had known how much God had already done, I would have felt differently. Although by the time I had arrived at the station the Deputy Governor had already left, the truth was his visit there had made a vital difference to my father's circumstances. I later found out that he had insisted formal procedures were carried out against my father. This was why my father was being questioned, so that he could be formally charged. Papa had already been held in a cell for more than twelve hours without anyone pressing charges against him. The Deputy Governor had insisted that Papa was either charged with a crime or released, and he had vowed to come back to check that correct procedures were being followed. His intervention had guaranteed my father's safety. Now that a Burundian official knew he was being held, it would be hard to make Papa 'disappear' without retribution of some kind.

Years later, I would have an even greater appreciation for the Deputy Governor's life-saving intervention, after my father relayed to me an incident during his first night in prison.

The day of his arrest, other men in his cell told my father they had seen new inmates taken away at midnight to be murdered. Hearing this, Papa had been terrified this was about to happen to him. He had stayed up all night, praying to God for his safety. Then, around midnight, two drunken guards approached his cell. They proceeded to have a loud argument that seemed to be about him. Their conversation was the most frightening thing he had ever heard.

'Why do I have to do this?' one said.

'Because it has been ordered,' the other replied.

'You do it, then.'

'No, I am not going to.'

'Go on . . . no one asked me directly. You can do it quickly.'

'No way. I won't.'

'Then let them do it themselves. I can't be bothered.'

'Okay, then, leave it. But I warn you, tomorrow the boss will be angry. You will be blamed.'

'Ah, who cares? We'll worry about that tomorrow.'

After that, the guards' footsteps had faded into the distance.

My father's relief was beyond words. He was certain his life had just been spared, at least for that night.

After the guards had walked away from his cell, my father told me he had given his life to Jesus. Before he had been a nominal Christian, but that night changed his life. He knew he might not have long to live and he felt he needed to have a right relationship with God.

At that moment, while I sat in the Gendarmerie feeling helpless to do anything for Papa, I didn't know what had taken place. I did not know then that God's saving and gracious hand was working things out in answer to my prayers, even when I could not see it.

I told the officer at the front desk I would wait in the lobby until my father had finished eating. I wanted to collect the empty container to use it for his meal the following day.

I watched another officer enter the room and assumed Papa was being asked more questions. Then, after a while, Papa was led to his cell again.

Minutes later, his empty food container was brought out to me. I left the Gendarmerie with a despairing heart.

Poor Papa! It was awful having to leave him there. I hoped we'd be able to speak more in the future if I continued to bring him his food each day.

I had been given permission to collect my father's bicycle from their custody room, so that Frédéric and I could ride it home. We rode quickly, eager to get back and relate everything to Mama.

As we travelled, we passed a river. I was thirsty so I told Frédéric we should stop so I could drink some water. Since I had Papa's food container in my hand, I decided to wash it after I had finished drinking.

Opening the container, I was surprised to find it wasn't empty. Mama had packed three sweet potatoes for Papa to eat but one of them still remained inside. This struck me as odd. A prisoner would be foolish to refuse to take all the food they were brought to eat. Papa could have saved it for later that day.

Why didn't he take it?

On closer inspection, everything became clear.

Turning the potato around, I noticed something had been wedged inside its orange flesh.

I pulled it out and saw it was part of a plastic bag wrapped around a piece of folded paper. Papa had written a message on the paper.

The words scrawled there were few but they were enough to make my stomach turn.

The note said: '*As soon as you see this, you and your brother Nixon must leave quickly. The officers plan to arrest you both.*'

And just like that, the plans I had made for myself evaporated once again.

I told Frédéric to return to Mama and warn Nixon right away. Then I took Papa's bicycle and did something I had vowed never to do again. I headed back to Tanzania and the refugee camp.

13

Escape

Exhausted and dejected, I arrived back in Mtabila the following morning. During my journey there, one question swam around in my mind.

What was I going to do now?

I had been forced to flee Burundi for the second time. Returning would be impossible now as the Army were looking to arrest me. But, after the incident with the disgusted Tanzanian driver, life in Tanzania would be unbearable, too.

The anguish I felt was immense.

Returning through the forest to enter the camp again, my will to live drained out through every pore of my body. In its place came a tormenting hopelessness.

I needed to accept the camp was the safest place for me now, but I just couldn't come to terms with it.

This time, when Thierry quizzed me about my absence, I chose to confide in him. I couldn't hold back my feelings any longer.

After describing what I had experienced in the past 48 hours, my frustrations came tumbling out: 'Thierry, we will die here if we do not try to get out of this place. I don't want to spend my whole life living in this camp. It is no life at all.'

'Yes, I know, Theo,' Thierry said. 'You are not the only one who feels this way. But what can we do?'

One option I had considered was to run away from the camp, pretend I was a Tanzanian, and take a job for any money I could get. I had picked up a lot of Swahili since coming to Tanzania and I knew I might be able to pass for a citizen if I tried hard enough. Then perhaps I could save my money and leave for a new country altogether, a country where I would be treated with respect and where my prospects might be different.

Before my experience of being called a bushman by the driver, I would never have dreamed of leaving behind the shelter, food and healthcare provided by the camp. Now I had an overwhelming feeling that I could stay there no longer. It wasn't simply because I could no longer endure the conditions and humiliation that I was forced to accept; part of me also felt I wasn't supposed to be in the camp any more.

Did God want me to be somewhere else? What did he want me to do? Would he direct me?

As I had cycled back to Tanzania that morning, thinking about everything that had just happened, I realised I could easily have been arrested the day I had visited my father at the Gendarmerie. I had been lucky to leave the police station and that Papa had managed to get a warning to me. Once again, I couldn't help but think God's intervening hand had been protecting my life. And the more convinced I was of this, the more I believed that God could not want me to stay in the refugee camp – that if I left it, God would continue to protect me.

I shared my thoughts with Thierry, certain he would laugh at me. Or maybe he would reassure me that in time I would calm down and feel differently.

His response caught me off-guard.

'You're right, Theo,' he said. 'Maybe it is time you left the camp . . .' He hesitated, then added: 'And I want to come with you.'

'You do, Thierry?' I said, wide-eyed. 'Are you being serious?'

'Yes . . . I am,' said Thierry. 'I cannot bear my life here, either. But I have a different suggestion altogether. I suggest we leave this country, too.'

'I don't understand,' I said. 'If we don't stay in Tanzania, where would we go?'

There was a glimmer in Thierry's eyes.

He lowered his voice to explain: 'I have been thinking about this for some time, but now that we can help each other, maybe we have a better chance . . . We'll save up some money from our work here and we'll go straight to Kenya. We'll have to smuggle ourselves across the border, but once we do, we should be okay. I have a cousin there who might let us stay with him. We'll live there and try to study again or maybe find ourselves some jobs. Then we can figure out what to do next.'

Excitement stirred inside me. This was a chance to make a new life for ourselves; a chance to escape the misery that had been our portion since the war in Burundi had begun.

Would we be successful? I didn't know the answer. But there was something I did know. This was an opportunity I couldn't decline.

'Let's do it, Thierry,' I said, feeling my face break into a smile. 'Let's plan to go to Kenya.'

Thierry grinned back at me.

'Yes, let's do it!' he said. 'We will save our money and leave when we have enough.'

We shook hands enthusiastically and laughed.

In that instant, my cloud of despair lifted.

I didn't have to stay in the refugee camp forever. Now I had a plan to give myself a future. I was determined it wouldn't fail. If Thierry and I could cross the Kenyan border illegally and locate his cousin, we were confident we could find a way to study again. Thierry's cousin was a senior pastor in the Methodist Church and they were known to give scholarships to needy students. Then, perhaps one day, we would be able to find jobs and earn the money we needed to build lives for ourselves.

I was convinced these opportunities outweighed any risks involved in leaving Mtabila. Even if we were caught leaving the camp and arrested, I knew I would rather face going to prison than risk spending the rest of my life there. At least that was how I felt at the time. As we contemplated our escape from the camp, it was a good thing we weren't able to foresee the future. For, if we had, we would have discovered the huge amount of trouble we were about to find ourselves in.

From that day onwards, life in the camp changed for me. With a clear goal in mind, I focused less on our circumstances and more on the task of saving money for our planned escape.

Along with my pay for being a Nursing Assistant, Thierry received a small wage for distributing medicines from an NGO called International Rescue Committee (IRC). We also made extra money by selling surplus rations we had. We intended to save enough to pay for our bus fares towards the Kenyan border, to secure a bribe to help get us across it and then to sustain us for several weeks afterwards.

Just a couple of days after my return to Mtabila, following the warning Papa had given us, my brother Nixon also arrived at the camp. I was thankful he had made it to Tanzania safely. Since our shelter was already full, I used some of my money to buy him a plot close to our own. This way, he could build his own settlement while remaining close to our group of boys.

Nixon soon found work, cooking in a makeshift café that had been set up. Despite my brother's presence in the camp, I wasn't deterred from the plan Thierry and I had made. We promised not to tell a soul about it, fearing the news would reach the authorities either before or after we had escaped Mtabila. It was hard to trust anyone in the camp. We also knew that our best attempt at success would be to keep the plan between the two of us. If we tried to take anyone else with us, there would be more chances of things going wrong. Because of this, Thierry didn't share our decision with his brother, Muzima, and I didn't tell Nixon, either. Nixon was not a risk-taker and I was confident he would be fine within the camp. If our plan to Kenya was successful, we intended to return and help our families with any finances we had.

Thierry and I knew we needed more than each other's help. After we had agreed to leave Mtabila, we started to seek God's presence and direction more fervently. We continued holding our daily prayer and weekly overnight meetings. We wanted to be sure God would be with us when we left, that he would protect us and give us success. Thierry was confident we were doing the right thing, but I started having doubts. This was because, for the first time in a long time, I felt that God had stopped speaking to me. I waited for a promise or verse from the Bible that would minister to my heart about God's purposes for me, but I never received anything. During our prayer meetings, some of the boys would feel God speak to them or offer prophecies for their fellow brothers. My revelation never came. Even so, I committed myself to praying about the journey to Kenya we were about to make. I hoped that when it happened, God would direct our steps as he had done so many times before.

Only later would I realise why God might have remained silent during that season. For the reality was, at that time, I wasn't yet ready to accept the path God had carefully mapped out for my life. How could I have understood that his plans would lead me to a future that would have seemed unthinkable to me at the time? The truth was, if God had revealed his plans for me, I would certainly have run away from him, too.

Months passed and conditions in the camp became more difficult for every refugee. We were already contending with problems based on the food rations we were given. The UNHCR provided us with maize and vegetable oil, not cassava flour and palm oil, as we were used to cooking with. This tempted us to go outside the camp to trade these foods for the ones we preferred, but this was illegal. Our rations of salt had stopped, too. Many were persuaded to undertake illegal activities, food smuggling or selling rations, as well as leaving the camp without permission, just so that we could stomach our meals. Others realised the best way to eat well in the camp was to have as many babies as possible, since child rations were the same as adult ones. The infant birth rate in the camp grew rapidly.

Then the UNHCR and Tanzanian Government issued a new rule regarding firewood. We were forbidden to obtain firewood from outside the camp, except on specific days, though the wood in the camp area had already been cut down and consumed. The official reason given was for the protection of the Tanzanian forest, but we wondered if this was to stop refugees from leaving the camp on the pretext of searching for firewood. Even when we were allowed to search for it, we were told we could only choose a tree that had fallen down by itself and had dried out. But here we were, more than a hundred thousand refugees in need of firewood to cook our meals. How could we all stumble across a dry tree that had fallen by chance? The probability of coming across such firewood was so slim, some refugees would have to walk or bicycle for miles and miles to find some, but it was illegal to travel outside a two-mile radius of the camp. Since Tanzanians were allowed to cut down trees, some refugees would arrange deals to have them felled in exchange for a payment. They would wait until they were dry to bring them into the camp. It was a tragic situation. Here we were surrounded by thousands of trees, yet in the camp, the number one, much-needed commodity became firewood. It felt like the UNHCR cared more about trees than us refugees and the difficulties we had to shoulder each day.

On top of this, Thierry and I began to experience more hardships when rebel groups within the camp started to harass us.

'You boys, don't waste your time in this camp,' they told us. 'You must come and fight with us! We have to go back to Burundi and save our people.'

There was a big rebel movement within the camp. Many disillusioned, traumatised and angry Hutus were keen to join it and the attempt to rid Burundi of 'Tutsi murderers'. Led by former Hutu politicians who had fled the country, the rebels would congregate after midnight, under the cover of darkness, to carry out military exercises with arms and weapons that had been smuggled in.

As much as our rational minds understood their cause and plight, Thierry and I were committed Christians and we knew we could not give in to their persuasions. God had already taught me so much about my need to forgive and move past the hatred and anger I had carried towards my Tutsi brothers. I couldn't ignore what he had shown me so clearly. We also knew from the Bible that Jesus asked his followers to be peacemakers. In our hearts we had a conviction that this was a better choice for us.

We were aware, however, that it would be only a matter of time before we landed ourselves in trouble with the rebels if we kept refusing their requests.

And so, feeling pressured, we hurried to set a date for our departure from the camp. We had been saving our wages for five months now and felt we had just enough to fund our trip to the Kenyan border, with a little left over. During the past months, we had also been busy making sure we were well-prepared for the journey ahead of us. We had befriended several Tanzanians who occasionally entered the camp and had elicited information from them regarding the timings of buses that ran closest to the camp and headed towards the Kenyan border. We knew of a bus route that would take us to it.

We had also bought ourselves material and sent it to a tailor in the camp to stitch in the style of typical Tanzanian clothing. The plan was to act as if we were Tanzanians. We knew we could get in trouble if people recognised we were not locals, so it was important to dress as though we were. If stopped, we planned to speak Swahili. We even obtained a couple of Tanzanian-styled hats that would add to our disguise. We chose names that were common in Tanzania to call each other. I would be 'Danford Bromera' and Thierry would be 'William Wilbert'.

In addition to our disguise, we would take one bag between us both, filled with a few sets of extra clothing. Thierry and I had big hopes of continuing our education in Kenya, so we also took our school certificates with us. Thierry had fled to Tanzania with his certificates and my father had brought some of his children's results slips with him when he had left Burundi. He had given my slip to me while we were in Heru-Ushingo together. Afraid that these pieces of paper might give away our true identities if we were stopped and searched, we had them sewn into the lining of the bag we would be carrying. The final thing we placed in our bag was a collection of medicines we had taken from the camp hospital. They included painkillers, Negram and anti-diarrhoea tablets.

With all these measures in place, we set a date to leave the camp. It was now October 1996. Almost three years had passed since I had first arrived in Tanzania. I was more than ready to leave the country and put all my hardships and frustrations behind me. Thierry and I were still very fearful we'd be caught fleeing the camp. If we were, we'd face imprisonment and then a return to war-torn Burundi. But life had beaten us down to the point where we were willing to accept this fate.

And so, one night around the stroke of twelve, when much of the camp was fast asleep, I gently shook Thierry awake.

'Come on, Thierry, get up!' I whispered. 'It's time to go.'

We quietly left our beds, picked up the bag we had prepared and made our way towards the forest that would take us away from the camp without having to leave the main entrance. My stomach churned with anxiety as we began our escape. Greater than anything else was my worry that our plan would not succeed. The hope of our escape from Tanzania had kept me going during the past five months. I was desperate for everything to go well.

I unleashed a torrent of requests to God as we finally left the forest and moved away from the perimeter of the camp.

Lord, protect us! Lord, let no one see us! Lord, please don't let your favour leave us!

It would be a two and a half mile walk to the bus stop where we'd catch the 6:30 a.m. bus to a town called Mwanza. Then we would board another bus towards the Kenyan border.

Lord, I don't know how we will make it across the border and what we will do when we reach Kenya, but I trust you will guide the way. Please stay with us and help this plan to work . . .

When Thierry and I finally spotted the bus stop, my fear began to abate. No one had seen or apprehended us. We were going to be okay. A little while longer and we would be on a bus far away from the camp and everything we had endured there.

Thierry pointed to a structure that stood a few metres back from the bus stop.

'Let's lie down in there and hide ourselves until morning,' he said. 'It's best we stay out of sight.'

The structure was a new brick building that was yet to be completed. The walls had been erected but it still lacked a roof. We entered through a door-less frame and lay down on the cement floor.

By now, it was 4 a.m. and a heavy feeling of fatigue hit me. While Thierry seemed alert and wide awake, I struggled to keep my eyes open.

'You could sleep anywhere and in any situation!' Thierry joked as he saw my fight to remain awake. 'Don't worry, rest for a while and I will keep watch.'

With his words of assurance, I closed my eyes and gave up my battle with exhaustion.

I opened my eyes again to a sky of light.

Where was the roof of our shelter?

It was morning and it took me a few moments to realise where I was.

No, we are not in the camp. I fell asleep at the bus stop.

Squinting because of the light, I sat up and turned to see where Thierry was.

Oh no. No way.

This can't be happening!

Suddenly, I was wide awake and fully aware of my surroundings.

For at that moment, standing right next to Thierry in our hideaway, was a police officer.

14

Caught!

We were in a mess. A terrible mess.

I couldn't believe this was happening to us.

The green khaki uniform and black, flat beret were the first things that caught my eye. I knew instantly that the figure who had joined us in our shelter was a Tanzanian policeman. I just didn't understand how he had managed to find us at that spot. He stood rifling through the bag Thierry and I had brought with us.

Turning to face me as he heard my waking movements, the officer held out the small boxes of medicines we had packed.

'Now your friend is awake, it is a good thing,' he said. He nodded his head towards me. 'Perhaps he can tell me what you are doing and why you are carrying these medicines with you. Smuggling items out of the camp is an illegal act.'

Just as I was glued to the spot, my mouth felt glued shut, too. What was I supposed to say in response? The officer appeared to know we were Burundian refugees from the UN camp, so how could I explain what we were doing sleeping at the bus stop? What was I supposed to say?

Thierry spoke up in Swahili.

'I told you, sir,' he said. 'We are just going to visit a friend. These medicines are ours . . .'

'You! Quiet!' The command made me jump. 'Let your friend speak.'

'Yes, it's true,' I uttered feebly. 'Just visiting a friend . . .'

My head was spinning.

We were finished. We were going to jail now. And then we would be sent back to Burundi.

I didn't understand how we could have been so unlucky. We hadn't even made it to the border.

Lord, I prayed that you would protect us, but you didn't! Where are you?

The policeman grabbed the medicines and placed them in his pocket. He handed the bag back to Thierry and ushered us outside. 'Okay, it's time to go back to the camp now,' he said. 'Come with me.'

He picked up a bike that had been lying on the ground. Grabbing the handles, he started walking ahead of us as he wheeled it alongside him.

As we walked a few steps behind him, our heads hung low in disbelief, he turned around slightly to tell us something.

'The camp has a small cell where you'll be held,' he said. 'I'm going to keep you in there until you can be transferred to the Tanzanian jail in Kasulu.'

His words filled us with terror. He didn't believe our story and it was unlikely anyone else would. We had gambled *everything* and lost. I had experienced hopelessness before, but now I sunk to an even greater depth. We were failures and even the God we had prayed to so earnestly had left us. We were going to be locked up in a prison cell, our freedom taken away from us. Then we would be forced to return to Burundi. And after that, who knew?

The events of the past three years, since the start of the war, replayed in my head as we followed the officer's steps. Yes, God had intervened in my life many times, saving me from death and doing great things in the midst of the great suffering we'd witnessed. But why had he done everything, if this was how my life was supposed to end? It didn't make sense. Had I just been imagining God's goodness to me? Had I fooled myself into believing God had a greater purpose for me?

Just then, the officer and his bike came to a halt, almost causing us to collide with him.

The officer was looking over to the other side of the road where there was another bus stop. Someone else seemed to be waiting there and he wanted to find out who it was.

Directing us over the road with him, the officer approached the man. As we drew closer, it was apparent the man was not a Tanzanian citizen either. He was dressed in a very conspicuous manner. He wore jeans and a bright T-shirt, with dark sunglasses and a heavy gold chain around his neck. Next to him was a large bulging sack.

'Hello, young man,' the policeman greeted him. 'And what are you are doing here? It looks like you are trying to go somewhere, too . . .'

The stranger had appeared deeply unsettled from the moment he spotted the policeman approaching him. He was shaking his head in what appeared to be regret and, as we drew closer, he started shifting from one foot to another in an agitated manner.

Replying in broken Swahili, he said: 'I am a refugee from Rwanda who was staying at the Rwandan camp. I was going to Kigoma to sell some plastic sheets. That's what's in my sack.'

I was taken aback by the man's honesty. The Rwandan refugee knew he was admitting to several illegal acts. He hadn't even attempted to cover his offences.

'Okay, then, sir,' the officer told the Rwandan, after opening the sack next to him to check its contents. 'Then you must come with me, too. Pick up your bag and walk along with these two men here. I will deal with all three of you together.'

The Rwandan joined Thierry and me as we crossed back over to the other side of the road, following the policeman and his bike as he headed in the direction of the UN camp.

I was startled at the refugee's honesty and compliance with the officer's requests. It was almost as he if didn't care that he was being arrested and was likely to end up in prison with us.

But my surprise didn't last for long when the Rwandan began to mutter something in Kinyarwanda to us as we walked along. Kinyarwanda was the official language of Rwanda. Because of its similarities to Kirundi, we were able to understand what he was saying. It was enough for us to realise the Rwandan's cooperative behaviour had really been an act.

'There are three of us and just one of him,' he said to us. 'Why can't we jump on the policeman and beat him up? Then we can all escape.'

I was astonished by his suggestion.

Attack a policeman? Was he being serious? Weren't we in enough trouble as it was?

I saw Thierry's horrified expression, too. Speaking up, I whispered back.

'No, we can't do that. It is not a good thing to do.'

The Rwandan seemed to shake his head in disgust.

'What cowards!' I heard him mutter.

His opinion of me was the last thing on my mind. I was still trying to grasp the reality of what was happening to us. There was no way out of this situation now. We couldn't use violence against another man just because we were desperate to escape.

Suddenly, the Rwandan grabbed the shoulder of the policeman and caused him to stop. Thierry and I froze where we were. What was he going to do?

'Wait! Listen, you!' the Rwandan said, forcing the officer to turn around to face him.

His tone was loud and menacing as he twisted his face into a sneer. 'I am a Rwandan fighter who has just left the war there,' he said. 'I'm not scared of anyone and I am not scared of you.'

My mouth fell open. Was he really challenging the policeman to a fight? Was this man crazy?

'Let me tell you what I am about to do,' he continued. 'I am going to close my eyes and if you are still there when I open them, you're going to have the same fate as all the other men I have fought against.'

The officer's eyes widened in horror.

Without saying another word, his quivering hands grabbed hold of the bars of his bike. He flung his leg over it and began to cycle away as fast as he could down the road.

I couldn't believe what I was seeing. The policeman had run away from the Rwandan and let Thierry and I go free.

My mind spun as I tried to process what would happen next. Was he going to report us and return with more officers? What were we supposed to do now?

As we were standing there, a loud rumble grew in volume as it approached us from along the road. The bus we had been waiting for was arriving. The Rwandan stretched out his hand to wave the bus to a stop. We saw the policeman, still cycling into the distance, looking back at us as the bus came to a halt where we were.

Thierry and I didn't move. Yes, the bus we needed was now in front of us, but were we really going to board it? Hadn't we just been arrested?

A hard thump on my back shoved me forward.

'Get on the bus, you two!' the Rwandan shouted. 'What are you waiting for?'

Thierry and I were in such a state of shock, we did as we were told. We climbed aboard.

The doors of the bus closed and it drove off towards Mwanza.

Sitting down on a bench, I noticed I was shaking uncontrollably.

Now that the Rwandan had threatened to kill the police officer and we had escaped arrest, were we in even greater trouble than we had been in before? Or was this God saving us?

I didn't know what to think.

Thierry and I were too scared to talk for the first 20 minutes of the journey. We were afraid the other passengers on the bus would become suspicious. When we were finally able to speak, we discussed our predicament in lowered voices.

'What do we do now?'

'Do you think the police will be pursuing us?'

'What if they intercept this bus? The officer saw us get on it.'

'Surely they don't care about us?'

'But if they arrest us again, we might be worse off than before. They might think we wanted to kill the policeman, too.'

Thierry and I were anxious the police would be searching for us and were tracking the bus we had boarded. Not wanting to take any chances, we disembarked at the next local town and spent the night at a hostel. The next day, we boarded another bus towards Mwanza and arrived there 11 hours later. After finding another small hostel to stay in, we caught a bus towards the border of Kenya the next morning. We were relieved that we had made it this far. By this time, I had decided God was helping us on our journey, just as we had prayed. Yes, when the policeman had found us, I had been quick to assume God had abandoned us. But how could I think that now, when God had used our impossible situation to show us just how powerful he was to save and protect us?

Surely he will help us across the border, too, even though we have to do it illegally, I thought. *He has shown us he is able to work miracles on our behalf.*

The journey by bus towards Kenya took six hours.

As we bumped and slid across our seats along the pot-holed route, we had ample time to think about the task before us.

A future in Kenya lay ahead, where we hoped to return to school or find jobs. But it depended on us being able to cross the border without being stopped.

We had been told there were local men we could find there who could be paid to help take us across. While there were immigration officers checking the documents of most people who crossed the border, there were also Tanzanian and Kenyan locals who crossed it daily without being stopped. If we could disguise ourselves as one of them, it would be easy to get across. But we needed help with this.

It was midday and the sun was hot by the time we arrived at the border. Getting down from the bus, we stood underneath the shade of the bus shelter as we scanned our surroundings. The border was a lively area, busy with people travelling in both directions. Connecting Kenya and Tanzania was a road about 200 metres long. On the Tanzanian side, a black metal gate had been erected to stop people crossing without passing through the immigration office block which stood on the right-hand side. Vehicles would have their papers checked at a barrier on the road, before it was lifted to let them pass. But there was also a smaller side gate that stood to the left of the border which had been left open. Here, locals who were passing by on foot or on bikes were allowed to come in and out without being stopped. They would pass through the little gate on the Tanzanian side, continue along the road connecting the two countries, and then leave through an open gate on the Kenyan side of the border which was unmanned.

Tanzanian immigration officers were posted at various points along the border's barriers, with several positioned outside the immigration block.

As Thierry and I stood waiting at the bus shelter, trying to figure out what we would do next, we noticed a couple of men headed towards us.

They had observed us waiting there and must have known we were looking for help of some kind.

'Let us help you, gentlemen,' one man said. 'Do you need to get across the border?'

Thierry and I looked at each other.

This was just what we had been hoping for.

'What can you do for us?' Thierry asked cautiously. 'We need to get to Kenya, but we cannot risk getting caught.'

The men explained they had a bike. One of them would ride it through the pedestrian gate while one of us sat behind him, as if we were a local, too. 'One of you can come with us and we will help the other find another bike to take him across.'

After negotiating a price, Thierry and I split up. It was agreed I would cross the border first with one of the men. Thierry would stay behind and be taken to another man who would help him follow soon after.

Climbing onto the back of the man's bike, my nerves were on edge.

I found myself holding my breath as he rode through the pedestrian gate, along with a group of other pedestrians and cyclists. No one called out to stop us. An immigration officer standing near the gate didn't even look up at us. Then we were cycling on the road between the two countries, joining the throng of other locals and travellers who were crossing the border. Though the journey felt like it took a lifetime, it must have taken less than three minutes. We reached the Kenyan pedestrian gate and got down from the bike to walk through it. Once again, no one stopped us. Within seconds, we were back on the bike and cycling away from the Kenyan border.

Thank you, God! Thank you! Thank you!

As we travelled away from the Kenyan gate, I felt overwhelmed with happiness. I almost wanted to laugh out loud.

I had made it across. I had done it. I was in Kenya now. The troubles of Burundi and the Tanzanian camp were now far behind me. I could hope for a better future in this new country.

Thierry will be here any minute now, I told myself. *We will celebrate together when he arrives.*

The man on the bike stopped after another few minutes of cycling and let me dismount by the side of a few small stores selling goods. Thierry had our backpack and most of our money but I had a few coins in my pocket and I thought I would buy myself a soda and wait for him to arrive.

I sat down on the road, enjoying my soda.

It was a hot day and it seemed especially refreshing. There was a light breeze blowing and it felt amazing against my skin.

After a few minutes, I caught sight of a man walking towards me.

I didn't recognise him, but he seemed to know who I was.

He walked right up to me and spoke quickly in Swahili.

Please tell me I'm not hearing this right! Please tell me I am dreaming!

'You should go now,' the man was saying. 'Get as far away from the border as you can or they will get you, too.'

The news he brought me was the worst I could have heard.

He explained Thierry had paid him to bring him across the border on his bicycle. They had just reached the Kenyan side when Thierry was stopped and questioned by a Kenyan immigration officer about his papers. When he hadn't been able to produce any, they had taken him into custody. Thierry had been caught!

Now this man was telling me I had to hurry away before I was found, too.

At that moment, I knew his plea made sense. Thierry was in big trouble now but I had made it over the border successfully. A future in Kenya was still mine to claim. But as I placed my soda down and stood up, I knew there was something else I needed to do. Every other option seemed inconceivable to me.

I thanked the man for his warning and then I turned towards the direction of the border. I started to walk back. I was about to hand myself in to the immigration authorities as well.

15

Behind Bars

I couldn't leave Thierry after everything we had shared and been through. It wasn't just the fact that he had our money and possessions. We had made our plan together and I couldn't imagine it succeeding without him. How could I go on to find a future in Kenya when I might never know what had happened to him?

I walked right up to the immigration block in Kenya and spoke to one of the officers in Swahili.

'My friend has just been caught trying to enter Kenya without papers. But I was with him, too, and I am not carrying papers, either. Please take me to him.'

The officers told me to leave them alone at first, refusing to believe I was serious. It took a few attempts before they finally agreed.

'If you want to be arrested,' they said, 'then it is your choice!'

They took me to an office where Thierry was being held. He sat across from another officer who had been questioning him.

Thierry looked up as I was brought in. His brow was spotted with perspiration and his face looked crumpled in defeat. I could tell he was terrified about the trouble he was in.

When he saw me walk in, a look of confusion appeared on his face. He had presumed I had made it across safely and couldn't understand how they had caught me, too.

The officer was writing down everything Thierry was saying.

'This man was with him,' the officer who brought me in said. 'You can take his statement, too.' He left the room shortly afterwards.

I was instructed to sit down next to Thierry.

'So, you are a Burundian refugee, too?' said the officer from across the table. 'Your friend has told me you were fleeing the war. Now, what do you have to say for yourself?'

Before I could speak, Thierry interrupted me.

'He speaks only Kirundi, sir,' he said. 'His Swahili is terrible. Let me translate between you both.'

Thierry spoke to me in Kirundi, pretending he was translating the officer's words to me. He knew the officer wasn't able to understand a word of Kirundi.

Instead, what he really said was: 'Theo, go along with what I am doing. Say something to me in Kirundi.'

'Uh . . . okay . . .' I said, doing as I was told. 'Well, I am not sure what to say. Let me know what story you told the officer.'

As Thierry pretended to translate between the officer and myself, he was able to tell me he had been questioned very harshly and so had admitted we had been trying to cross the border illegally. But he had told the officer we had come straight from Burundi. He hadn't confessed we had been living in the Tanzanian refugee camp. International refugee laws dictated refugees could only claim asylum in the first country they fled to, and it would have been worse if they had discovered we had been living in the UN camp and had left it illegally.

Thierry pretended my statement in Kirundi matched what he had told the officer. It was important we didn't reveal we had left the camp.

After I had been questioned, Thierry and I were escorted back through Kenyan immigration. They walked us along the road we had travelled by bicycle.

They were returning us back to Tanzania.

We were handed over to the immigration authorities there.

On the way, I managed to have quick snatches of conversation with Thierry.

'How did you get caught?' he asked me. 'I had hoped you had made it.'

'I came back when I realised they had taken you,' I said. 'I couldn't leave you to get in trouble by yourself.'

'You are a good friend, Theo, but we will both be punished now.'

'Do you think they will put us in prison?'

'I am hoping they'll just send us back to the UN camp. They have no proof we were ever there.'

'It's a good thing the Tanzanian police officer took our medicines,' I said, suddenly realising our good fortune. 'If they had searched your bag and found them, they would have known where we had come from.'

In spite of this, our minds were still clouded with fear.

We had no idea what would happen to us now.

Just an hour earlier, I had been celebrating my entry into Kenya, believing our plan had succeeded. But here we were back in Tanzania and in trouble again.

It felt like a cruel joke was being played on us.

God, are you punishing or helping us? What are you doing?

I didn't know if I should keep praying that God would somehow intervene again, or if I should just accept that he had let us fail. I didn't even have the strength to hope any more.

Two Tanzanian officers questioned Thierry and me. We repeated our story so that another statement could be recorded.

Then a new man entered the room. Unlike the blue-shirted immigration officers, this man wore a dark, short-sleeved suit. The immigration officers stood up when he entered the room. It was obvious he was a senior officer.

'Have you finished with their statements?' the suited man asked the officers. 'I have time to look at them now.'

We watched as the officers handed some papers to him and followed him out of the room.

I glanced at Thierry.

'What do you think they are going to do with us?'

'Who knows?' he sighed. 'I think that man is making a decision about us.'

When the two officers returned shortly afterwards, we were told to stand up.

'Come on,' one officer said. 'It's time to go.'

We were led outside and escorted to a car.

Before we climbed in, the officer said: 'We understand you have problems in Burundi and we will try to help you. You are going somewhere where you can rest.'

His statement gave us some hope.

'They must be taking us back to the camp,' I whispered to Thierry once inside the car. 'They are taking pity on us and returning us there.'

'I hope you're right,' Thierry said. 'It would be the best outcome for us.'

The ride took half an hour. But when the car stopped, we realised we had arrived at a police station.

Once inside, we were given orders in Swahili.

'Remove your belt.'

'Take off any metal objects.'

'Hand over your bag, we will keep it.'

It didn't take long for it to dawn on us that we weren't being taken back to the camp after all.

Instead, we had been arrested.

A police officer told us we were being charged with entering Tanzanian territory illegally. Since we claimed we had come directly from Burundi, but had failed to notify Tanzanian authorities that we were seeking asylum while travelling to Kenya, our presence in Tanzania had breached the law. We would be held in custody until our case was heard in court.

We were distraught beyond words. Our worst fear had come true. We had ended up in prison.

Our cell was a small, dark, cement-walled room. It was completely bare apart from a single plastic bucket in the corner and another inmate who was already inside. A small amount of light seeped in through a thin opening placed high up towards the ceiling. Since it was already six in the evening, this light was fading fast. As the thick metal door of the cell closed behind us, Thierry and I sunk to the floor in exhaustion. We hadn't eaten all day and I had bad hunger pains. But the physical discomfort we felt was nothing compared to the emotional distress we were in.

We had no idea how long we would have to remain behind bars until our case would come to court. It could take months. And if we were found guilty, we would face even more time in prison.

We had risked an escape to Kenya knowing we might land ourselves in prison. But now we had actually been placed in a cell, the reality seemed a hundred times worse.

Inmates in Tanzanian prisons, just as in Burundi, were only given water to sustain them. It was left up to family and friends to provide them with food. But Thierry and I had no one to help us here. I didn't know how we would survive.

We were afraid to say much to each other. We didn't know who the other inmate in the cell was and we were afraid he might understand us if we talked in Kirundi and report what we said back to the officers.

A few hours after we'd been locked up, the metal door to our cell swung open and a new officer we hadn't seen before appeared.

He looked over at us as if he had found something disgusting on the sole of his shoe. The coldness in his small black eyes alarmed me.

What did he want?

'I thought you must need some water,' he said, smirking. 'One of you come with me to get some.'

Thierry offered and returned a few minutes later with two buckets of water. But after Thierry had brought them back, the officer did something cruel. Picking up the buckets, he threw the water across the floor of the cell, splashing every corner.

He chuckled to himself.

'Try to get some sleep,' he said to us. 'Soon I will return to give you a good beating as your welcome present.'

He chuckled again and I wondered if he had been drinking. Then he was gone, slamming the metal door behind him.

It unnerved us greatly. Not only could the three of us not sleep well because of the damp floor, but now Thierry and I were terrified the officer would return to beat us up.

This was a nightmare. How could God allow us to go through this after everything we had been through? At that moment, I would have done anything to be back at the UN camp again.

I should have just joined the rebels when I was asked to, I thought bitterly. *Then we wouldn't be in this situation. God doesn't care for us at all.*

We barely slept that night. We jumped at every noise we heard, hoping it wasn't the officer returning to beat us.

Eventually morning broke. Thankfully, the officer had not returned to trouble us that night.

Instead, when the cell door opened again, we were ushered out by a new and senior officer. He handed us a loaf of bread.

'Here, eat this,' he said. 'You men must be hungry.'

Thierry and I glanced at each other, surprised by his kindness.

We consumed our pieces of bread as if it was the best meal we had ever eaten.

The Tanzanian officer spoke to us as we ate.

'You are being moved from this prison to another,' he said. 'You will leave in a few minutes.'

With two police officers escorting us, we were taken outside and placed on a bus headed towards Mwanza. Fifteen minutes into the journey, the policemen urged us to get off.

We had arrived at a larger police facility.

After being searched, we were taken to our new cell.

As the door opened, I was overcome by the smell of urine and human waste. Our new cell was perhaps three metres by four, but there were five other men there to share the space with us. The floor was so dirty and stained, I didn't know how I would bring myself to sit down on it, even though a few of the men were happily lying across it.

This place is ten times worse than the last one! I thought to myself. *What will we do now?*

Little did I know, my first impression could not be trusted.

For even when I felt like God had abandoned us to a wretched fate, he was preparing to amaze us again with his goodness.

Our experience in this new prison cell would turn out to astound us in ways we could not have imagined.

The first thing we didn't expect was how quickly we were welcomed by our new cellmates. They were interested in getting to know us.

'Where are you from?'

'Why are you here?'

'What are they charging you with?'

We told the men our names and shared part of our story about our flight from Burundi. In turn, the men introduced themselves and shared information about their lives. One inmate was a judge who had been accused of accepting a bribe. Another told us he was being charged with murder. One confessed he had been caught with drugs.

Before we had entered the cell, the bag we had fled the camp with had been searched and returned to us. Remembering we had a couple of cans of tinned fish and some biscuits inside, I brought them out to eat as we talked.

'Please share this with us,' I said, offering the opened tins and biscuits to the other men.

As we all ate and chatted, one of the inmates said: 'You men have no family to feed you but you are sharing all the food you have with us. Now you need not worry, we will take care of you, too.'

Thierry and I were overwhelmed with the fraternity between the men in the cell. They seemed to go out of their way to help and support each other and wanted to do the same with us, too. The judge told us he would give us advice to help us when we had to go to court. Another inmate refused to let us empty the plastic bucket we used as a toilet.

'You men are just visitors here,' he said. 'We can't let you do that.'

Here we were, incarcerated with men who had broken the law and carried out awful crimes, but we felt like we were with family.

The following day, something even more incredible happened.

An officer arrived at the door with two food packages in his hand. He handed them to Thierry and me.

'Your sister brought these for you,' he said.

'Sister?' I said. 'Which sister is that? Who is she?'

'Just eat!' we were told and the officer left the room.

Inside the food parcel was a meal of meat, milk and bread.

It was truly one of the most delicious meals I had ever eaten. We were amazed.

When the food packages continued to arrive three times a day without fail, I just couldn't deny something I had been struggling to believe.

God did care about us! And he was providing for us, just like he had done before!

Though we asked to meet the lady who was bringing us food every day, the officers denied us the privilege. They wouldn't tell us her name, who she was or how she had known we were in prison without relatives to help us.

It was a wonder that a stranger could show us such kindness.

I had been so angry at God for allowing us to get arrested and put in prison when we had been so close to reaching Kenya. I had been convinced he had cruelly left us to a miserable fate. But how could I continue to think this way when Thierry and I were being overwhelmed with such care and help? Our time in prison should have been the worst time of our lives, but instead the inmates encouraged us and we continued to be well fed.

I was reminded of the Old Testament story of Joseph who was imprisoned but was still blessed by God who helped him find favour there. We, too, had found such favour.

Yes, our cell was filthy and we craved a clean shower, but our spirits were comforted with a sense of hope about our predicament. Our new friends assured us that our case was not a severe one. The judge advised us that if we pleaded guilty to the charges against us, expressed our remorse and explained what we had suffered in Burundi, the court judges might even let us off with a fine.

Thierry and I were told we had a court hearing date set for two weeks after we had arrived. Now, we began to hope that we would be released and might even be permitted to return to the camp. God may have allowed us to go to prison, but hadn't he shown us he was still with us? Wouldn't he continue to help us?

As our court date grew closer, we prayed fervently about the outcome.

Lord, I don't understand your ways, but it's impossible for me to believe that you aren't with us. Please don't abandon us in that courtroom.

And so we waited to appear before the judges who would decide our fate, hoping that God would intervene once again.

16

Case Closed

On the day of our court hearing, at 10 a.m. that morning, Thierry and I were led out from our cell to a courthouse that was a half-mile walk away from the station. Though we weren't restrained with handcuffs, we had been issued four police officers to escort us on the way.

Of course, we were very troubled over what would happen that day. Since we had no money we could not afford a defence lawyer, so we would have to argue our case for ourselves. By following the advice from our judge inmate, we hoped we would find the favour we needed. Although Thierry and I had been praying God would also help us escape serious punishment, the truth was we were still terrified about the outcome.

God has done so much for me already, I tried to reassure myself. *Even when I have doubted him, he has always been there for me. I must keep trusting him . . .*

The hearing was to take place in the largest courtroom. Since our case was the first to be heard, we were led straight inside just minutes after our arrival.

Sitting at an imposing wooden desk at the front of the courtroom were three judges. All three wore long black robes with white scarf ties at their necks. I noticed the judge sitting in the middle, presumably the presiding judge, appeared to be much older than the other two. To the right of their desk was a smaller desk where a court clerk was positioned. On a platform slightly lower than the judges, a prosecutor sat at a table, reading through some papers. Next to him was one of the Tanzanian immigration officers who had taken our statements after we'd been caught. Opposite these men, and to the left of the judges, was a wooden dock. On a third and lower platform were a dozen or so benches, half-filled with spectators. As we entered the courtroom, we were led straight to the front bench and told to sit down. I assumed those sitting behind us were the friends and family of other men and women who were waiting for their hearing.

'Thierry Bahizi and Theodore Mbazumutima, your case will be first,' the presiding judge's voice started the proceedings. 'Please approach the dock to commence. I am going to read out the charges against you both.'

Thierry and I cast anxious glances towards each other as we stood up.

We had been waiting for our trial for two weeks. Our futures depended on everything that took place at this hearing.

We climbed onto the first platform and positioned ourselves behind the dock.

'Thierry Bahizi and Theodore Mbazumutima,' the judge continued. 'You are here today on the following charges. Count one, you are charged with entering Tanzania illegally. Count two, you are charged with entering the country without identifying yourself to the proper authorities. Charge three . . .'

I almost gasped aloud when I heard the third charge that was being held against us. We hadn't expected this at all . . .

'. . . you are charged with attempting to spy in our country.'

Thierry and I were still pretending that I could not understand Swahili. He had been given permission to translate between the court and me and was repeating the prosecutor's words to me in Kirundi.

As he relayed the count to me, I shook my head in disbelief. Thierry looked equally stunned.

The accusation was astonishing. How could they think we were spies?

If we were found guilty of being spies, there was no doubt we would face a lengthy spell in prison. How had they come to that conclusion? I was certain the court had no evidence to prove we were spies. But after hearing this charge, I was also afraid that the judges or prosecution were corrupt. If this was the case, we were in big trouble.

The presiding judge invited the prosecutor to come forward to present any evidence he had regarding these charges. The prosecutor stepped out from behind his table and called the Tanzanian immigration officer to join him. After introducing him to the court, he asked the officer to read out the statement he had taken from us after we had been caught at the border.

'You see,' the prosecutor addressed the judges, 'these men have entered Tanzania illegally and I believe they were aware of what they were doing, contrary to what you have heard them say in the statement they gave. I believe they are actually *Banyamulenge* from the Democratic Republic of Congo and they have come here to spy on the activities in this region of Tanzania . . .'

The accusation was so ridiculous, I wanted to laugh out loud. The *Banyamulenge* were a Tutsi tribe who were currently opposing the Government in Congo's fierce civil war. Thierry and I were aware of the rumours circulating that this tribe also intended to claim land in Tanzania.

'Don't you see how these men are tall? And just look at their features!' he continued. 'They cannot be Burundian Hutus like they claim, they must be *Banyamulenge* and that is why they have no good reason to explain how they crossed the border from Tanzania to Kenya without realising what they were doing . . .'

Other than the observations he was making about our appearance, the prosecutor had no other evidence to bring against us regarding the charge of us being spies. I wished we had documentation on us to prove that we really were Burundian Hutus. Would the court believe what the prosecutor was saying? That we were really Tutsis . . . and spies at that?

'How do you plead?' I heard the presiding judge's voice demand. He addressed his question to Thierry first.

Our judge friend had advised us to plead guilty to the charges of entering the country illegally. But he had told us we should ask for the opportunity to explain ourselves. Now I wondered if this could really help us.

As for the accusation of being a spy, what could we say to convince them that we weren't?

Thierry was quick to respond on behalf of both of us.

'Your Excellencies,' he said, 'it is true that we are both guilty of entering Tanzania illegally. We would both like to plead guilty to the first two charges. But there is no truth to the charge of us being spies.' He paused, then added, 'And if the court gives me an opportunity, I would like to explain our actions and why we entered here illegally.'

The presiding judge nodded his consent: 'You may address the court.'

I waited as Thierry seemed to collect his composure. I wondered what he was going to say. Was there really anything we could tell the court to justify our actions? Would they understand?

Then I heard his voice begin to describe what he had experienced at the onset of the war.

He said: 'We are very sorry that we breached the law. But we are not criminals or even spies. We are just people who need help. There is a war now in our country Burundi and because of it, some Tutsi men came to kill me and my family. They burned our house down and I even watched as my little nephew was attacked with a machete . . .'

As Thierry spoke, his voice choked.

Tears started to spill from his eyes.

Though he was weeping, he continued to recount his experiences of the war to the judges.

And that's when I noticed something unbelievable happening.

At first I thought I wasn't seeing correctly. But then, I realised I was.

The presiding judge, who wore glasses, was lifting up the rim of his spectacles. He seemed to be wiping something away from under his eye.

Was he crying, too?

Before Thierry had finished recounting his whole story, the judge held up his hand.

'It's okay,' he said. 'You can stop there. Now, please invite your friend to explain his actions to us, and you may translate for him to the court.'

Thierry looked at me and repeated the judge's request to me in Kirundi.

Now it was my turn to help the judges understand what we had been through.

Aware that they had been affected by Thierry's account, I knew I had to share the painful experiences I had suffered, too. I began to speak in Kirundi, pausing frequently for Thierry to translate. Though I could not mention our time in the UN camp, I described the moment I had fled from my school and encountered both the Hutu and Tutsi mobs who wanted to take my life. I shared how I had found my family's home ransacked and the dread I felt wondering if they were still alive. Then I spoke about the time I became separated from my sister Christine, as the Army had fired rounds into my grandparents' village. And how I later learned that many from my extended family had burned to death in a hut that had been set on fire.

The judge held up his hand again.

'Thank you,' he said. 'You may both sit down.'

As we sat on our bench again, we watched as all three judges bowed their heads to confer in lowered voices. After a few minutes, the presiding judge cleared his throat to speak.

'Thierry Bahizi and Theodore Mbazumutima . . .' his voice beckoned. 'We have heard both sides regarding the charges and a decision has been made regarding them . . .'

I held my breath.

What would happen to us now?

'Regarding the first charge against you of entering Tanzania illegally . . . we find you guilty. As for the second charge of entering the country without identifying yourself and the third charge of entering the country to spy . . . you are both found not guilty.' He added: 'And as a consequence of you breaching the law, the court orders you to pay a fine of 11,000 Tanzanian shillings each. We also order you both to leave Tanzania within the next 24 hours . . .'

Bam!

His wooden hammer hit the desk.

'This matter is closed. Please exit the court.'

Relief washed over me. Our punishment was to be a fine, not imprisonment!

I was certain I could still see tears in the judge's eyes as he proclaimed our sentence.

It was incredible. The judges had been moved by our stories and taken pity on us. We had escaped jail and would be released after paying our fine.

It was over. And we were free men.

I took a moment to praise God in my heart.

This could only be because of you! Thank you for helping us!

The judges weren't corrupt after all. Instead they had been sympathetic to our plight.

I felt like jumping for joy. The sentence we had been given was the best thing we could have hoped for. The money we had left in our possession was also a little over what we needed to cover the fine.

As we left the courtroom, an officer told us he would escort us to the office where we needed to pay our fine.

While we were on our way, we heard a voice call out to us.

'Hold on there, men! Can I talk to you?'

We stopped walking and turned around to discover the voice belonged to a young lady. I recognised her as one of the spectators who had been inside the courtroom, as she was particularly beautiful. She wore a fitted patterned dress and her shiny black hair was styled into a pretty crop.

We didn't know who she was but we paused to hear what she had to say.

'I heard everything you told the judges about your lives,' she said, 'and I am so sorry for what you have both experienced. I just wanted to know if you had the money to pay the fine?'

I wondered why she appeared so concerned about us.

'Yes, thank you for your care,' Thierry answered. 'We have the money to pay.'

The lady smiled at us and nodded. 'I am glad,' she said.

Thierry and I continued on to the office to pay the fine. It left us with little money to spare, but we would have to worry about that later. We were also handed a piece of paper.

We left the building and stepped outside before we stopped to inspect what was written on the document.

After reading what it said, our happiness dissolved.

It was a notice which stated our release from prison. It also stated that we had to leave Tanzania within 24 hours.

I had forgotten about this part of the sentence handed down to us.

'What are we going to do now?' I said to Thierry. 'How can we leave Tanzania? Where will we go?'

The only practical option we had was to leave the country and enter Kenya. But we couldn't attempt to cross the border illegally again, especially since we had already been stopped by the immigration authorities there. Even if we had tried to reach Burundi, there was no way we could reach our country's border within 24 hours. It was too far away. Unless we flew out of Tanzania, it would be impossible to leave as we had been ordered. But we had no funds to pay for flights.

'If we stay in Tanzania, they will put us back in prison again,' Thierry said. 'I am at a loss to suggest a solution.'

We had found ourselves in yet another impossible situation.

'Where are you both headed to now?'

The question which interrupted our conversation came from a familiar voice.

It was the same lady who had asked us about our fine inside the courthouse. She had just joined us outside.

'Oh . . . we are not sure,' I told her. 'It seems like we can't go anywhere.'

'What problems do you have?' she said. 'Maybe I could help?'

I was hesitant to reveal too much, but at the same time we were also quite desperate. Trying to be cautious, I explained our dilemma to the lady in Swahili. Now our court case was over, I could stop pretending I could only speak Kirundi.

'I see,' the lady said after she had listened. 'So, please tell me, if you had a choice, what would you want to do?'

'We had hoped to get to Kenya,' I told her. 'That's where we really want to be.'

'If that's the case,' she said, 'do you need someone to get you there?'

I hesitated for a second. Was she saying she could help us cross the border?

'We may do,' I said, still uncertain about her intentions. 'Do you know anyone?'

The lady's eyes seemed to smile at me.

'Yes,' she said. 'I think I do. Now come, follow me . . .'

Thierry and I didn't know what to think.

Who was this stranger and why did she want to help us? It didn't make any sense. Could we trust her?

Shrugging his shoulders, Thierry looked at me.

'What other option do we have, Theo?' he said. 'Let's go.'

I couldn't argue with Thierry. If we were to avoid prison again, we needed to accept any offer of help we could find.

We followed the lady as she led us away from the courthouse, back along the route we had taken from the police station. She said nothing more to us as we walked and we didn't dare to ask who she was and where she was taking us.

Just 15 minutes later, we arrived at another large building, an old colonial structure which had been transformed into an office base. But there were no signs posted that told us what type of business or organisation was operating here.

We walked into a spacious hall with a reception desk. The hall was attached to several office rooms. The lady told us to sit down and wait for her and then she went up to a door and knocked on it.

'Yes, come in,' a voice said, and she entered. As she did so, she left the office door wide open.

We were able to look inside the room and, when we did, we saw her walk towards a man sitting behind a cluttered desk.

'Oh my goodness, Thierry!' I said when I caught sight of him. 'That is the same man from the border.'

In a similar, short-sleeved suit, was the senior immigration office who had reviewed our statements at the Tanzanian border. I was sure he was also the man who had ordered us to be sent to prison.

'These offices must belong to the Tanzanian Immigration,' I realised suddenly. 'And she must be talking to him about us!'

I was stunned by what I was seeing. Our lady friend approached the officer and greeted him with what seemed to be a familiar hug. They began to talk and their conversation appeared very jovial. Was our lady friend really asking this man to help us? But wasn't he the man who had sent us to prison in the first place? What was her relationship to him?

Ten minutes must have passed before the lady finally turned around to exit the room. The senior officer followed her out, too. Though we had been watching her conversation with the officer, we had no idea what they had been discussing. The lady brought the officer out to us and we stood up respectfully to greet him.

Then she made an announcement that caught Thierry and I by surprise.

'I am leaving now, but follow this man and he will help you,' she said. 'I have arranged everything.'

Arranged everything? What had she arranged for us?

I couldn't understand why a stranger had gone to so much trouble to help us. Had our story really moved her that much?

We grabbed the opportunity to thank her for what she had done.

There seemed to be no reasonable explanation for our stroke of luck, though at the back of my mind was a conviction that this wasn't luck at all.

God's hand must be in this!

I was blown away by everything that was happening to us at that moment.

Before we knew it, the lady had turned around to walk out of the immigration headquarters.

It was the last time we ever saw her.

17

On to Nairobi

'We must leave now,' the senior officer told us. 'Come along with me.'

It was already growing dark outside and the office would be shutting down soon.

He led us to his car and asked us to get inside. Then he climbed into the front seat and started driving.

Where was he taking us?

Thierry and I didn't say a word between us. We had no idea what would happen next and were too scared to ask the officer any questions. The whole situation seemed surreal to me.

When the car pulled up in front of a small brick house, we realised the officer must have taken us to his own home.

A lady, whom we assumed was the officer's wife, opened the door to us.

'Put some hot water out for a bath,' the officer told her. 'These men will bathe.'

He led us to a bedroom and told us we could change our clothes there after we had washed.

We bathed and came out of our room to find a hot meal ready for us on the kitchen table.

The kindness we were being shown was unexpected. Even while we were in his house, we couldn't be sure of the officer's intentions towards us. He still hadn't told us a thing about how he planned to help us.

As we were eating, the officer encouraged us to finish our meal quickly.

'We have to get to the border soon,' he said. 'I will take us there.'

Thierry and I exchanged looks.

Was the immigration officer really going to help us get to Kenya?

Before long, we set off in the officer's car again. Within 20 minutes, we had arrived back at the Tanzanian and Kenyan border where we had been apprehended.

What happened next was incredible to us both. Everything that took place seemed like a dream.

The senior immigration officer brought us inside the immigration office and went behind a desk there. He brought out two passes and wrote something down on them. As he handed them to us, I noticed he had written a statement declaring us to be students from Tanzania who were travelling via Nairobi, the Kenyan capital, to reach another place in Tanzania called Arusha (since Arusha was only accessible by transiting through Kenya first).

Taking us through the immigration block in Tanzania, the officer then proceeded to walk us along the road towards the Kenyan border. He waited while a Kenyan immigration officer there stamped our passes and then he walked out with us onto Kenyan soil.

'This way, men,' the officer said and led us to a bus depot that had several coaches filling up with passengers. Reaching into his pocket he brought out two paid tickets for a bus headed towards Nairobi.

'These are yours,' he said, 'and I think your bus is over there. It leaves at 10 p.m. tonight.'

We were speechless. How could we comprehend what had just happened?

We were in Kenya now, just as we had hoped and dreamed. And we had been able to walk cross the border with no trouble at all. And on top of all this, it was a senior immigration officer from Tanzania who had just helped us get there.

'Thank you so much, sir!' I said to the officer, shaking his hand vigorously. 'You have helped us so much. We can't thank you enough!'

Thierry shook his hand too, reiterating my words of gratitude.

'No problem, men,' he replied quite simply. 'Luck be with you . . .'

Then he turned around to head back towards Tanzania.

As we watched him walk away from us, I felt overwhelmed by the awesomeness of God.

It was just under three weeks since we had left the UN camp. During that time, we had been caught and arrested twice on our way to Kenya. We had been taken to jail and released and then found ourselves in a crisis when we had been ordered to leave Tanzania within 24 hours. But God had rescued us from all these predicaments. He had used prisoners to encourage us and give us advice about our trial. He had used a stranger in the courthouse to offer us the help we needed. He had even used the same immigration officer who had sent us to jail to get us across the border. It was just incredible.

'Thierry, our God is so faithful and good!' I said as we sat ourselves down on the bus we were to take. 'He is just so amazing! How will anyone ever believe what he has done for us?'

'I don't think I believe it myself,' he said. 'Are we really in Kenya now? Did we really make it here after everything we've been through?'

We laughed together, shaking our heads in bewilderment as we thought about everything we had experienced and witnessed together.

Once again, we were uplifted by a strong sense of hope. If God had done so much for us already, surely our future in Kenya would be promising, too?

We were now travelling to Nairobi to find Thierry's cousin. He did not know we were coming and we had no address for him, but Thierry was confident we would be able to find him easily since he was a pastor and a deputy to the Bishop in the Methodist denomination.

'When we arrive in Nairobi, we will just find a Methodist church and find out where he is,' Thierry assured me. 'It shouldn't be so difficult.'

Just after six in the morning, the bus arrived at Kenya's capital city.

We gazed out of the bus window with wide eyes. The city was far bigger than we had imagined. In fact, it was huge! It seemed to be crammed with buildings and people. As the bus travelled through the busy roads on its way to the main depot, we were daunted by the task ahead of us. Perhaps we had underestimated how difficult it would be to find Thierry's cousin in such a big city.

Descending from the bus, Thierry reached inside his bag and brought out the remainder of the money we had. We had managed to exchange our Tanzanian shillings for Kenyan ones and now had 260 Kenyan shillings (roughly £2) between us both.

It wasn't much at all. We would need to find Thierry's cousin soon if we wanted to have a place to stay and food to eat.

Spotting several taxis waiting, Thierry suggested we approach one and ask to be taken to a Methodist centre or church where we could get more information.

'I know of a Methodist guest house that's not too far away,' the taxi driver told us. 'I can take you there.'

The taxi ride cost us 220 shillings. This meant we had 40 shillings left in our pockets when we climbed out of the taxi.

'I hope someone can help us here,' I said to Thierry as we entered the guesthouse. 'If not, we'll end up sleeping on the road.'

'Good morning, can I help you?' said the receptionist at the front desk, addressing us in Swahili.

'Yes, you can,' said Thierry. 'We are looking to find a Methodist pastor called Jean Kabura. Do you have any information on how we can find him?'

The lady reached for a book lying on her desk and began leafing through it.

Inching her finger across a list of names, she furrowed her brow.

'No, I am afraid there are no guests staying here by that name.'

'Oh no,' said Thierry. 'You misunderstand. He is not one of your guests. He is a Methodist pastor who also happens to be a Burundian like us. You must know him, he is the deputy of Bishop Kariuki.'

'Oh!' the lady said. 'Well, I'm very sorry. I haven't heard of him, or the Bishop, either. I think these men belong to the United Methodist Church. But we are the Free Methodist Church. We are actually a different denomination.'

Thierry's face fell.

We had just spent the last of our money on getting to the guesthouse but it had been a complete waste.

'Is there anything else I can do for you?' the lady asked, sounding impatient. 'Would you like to book a room?'

'Er . . . no thanks,' said Thierry, turning towards me. 'My friend and I will stay elsewhere. But are you sure you have no information to help us find this man?'

The receptionist seemed suspicious of us and our reasons for being there. Sensing her unease, we were about to leave, when she made a suggestion.

'I have another Burundian guest staying here today. His name is Jerome. Should I call him to meet you? I can't help you, but maybe he can.'

We waited as she dialled a number and put the phone to her ear. After a voice at the other end answered, she said: 'I have two men from Burundi with me now. They have asked to speak to you.'

She handed the phone to Thierry.

'Yes, hi,' said Thierry, speaking in Kirundi. 'My name is Thierry Bahizi and I am a refugee from our country. I am looking for my cousin who is in this city. His name is Jean Kabura. He is a Burundian, too. I wondered if you might know him or know anyone who could help us find him?'

Seconds later, Thierry put the phone down.

'He said he's coming down to meet us now, Theo. Let's pray he knows someone who can help.'

Jerome turned out to be a tall, grey-haired man. Dressed in a smart blue suit, he strolled up to us and greeted us with a smile and a handshake.

'So what problem do you have, gentlemen?' he asked.

'We need to find my cousin,' Thierry explained. 'We are refugees who have fled the war and we have just arrived in Kenya today. We have nowhere else to go and no money left on us. Is there any way you can help us find him?'

'Well,' began Jerome, 'when I heard the name you mentioned, I was quite surprised. You see, I only came to Kenya for a few weeks to complete some research I am doing. I actually leave for Europe tomorrow. But of the few Burundians I have met while staying here, Jean happens to be one of them.'

'You know him?' I asked incredulously. 'So you know where he lives, too?'

'Yes, in fact, I do,' the man said cheerfully. 'And I can take you to him, if you wish.'

Thierry and I were amazed. We were certain this was another display of God's faithfulness at a time when we were fully dependent on him. I knew I would never be able to forget the love and goodness God had showered upon us. How could I ever deny how awesome and powerful he was? He was a living God who cared about his children and was able to do great things for them, just as the Bible promised.

A few hours later, after Jerome kindly escorted us by bus, we arrived at the home of Thierry's cousin.

Jean was surprised to see us standing outside his door. But he welcomed us in.

'I don't think there is room for you here,' he told us regretfully as we explained we had nowhere else to go. 'But let me speak to my neighbour and see if they can take you in.' It was true, his house was very small. Since he had eight children and a wife to care for, it was already very crammed. His neighbour agreed to let Thierry and I sleep in their spare room. But we were told we had to find our own place within two months.

After risking everything to enter Kenya, this certainly wasn't the future we had envisioned for ourselves. We had no money, no means of earning a living, and we knew our accommodation would be temporary. But we were sure of one thing – God must have wanted us in Kenya as he had done so much to get us there. We had to trust he would provide for us, just as he had provided for us before. So we decided to do everything possible to sustain ourselves in Kenya.

And as we realised there were many things that we needed which lay out of our reach, we turned our focus towards God and waited to see what he would do.

18

God's Provision

Now that we had arrived in Kenya, we needed permission to stay. Our first priority was to apply for refugee status from the UNHCR. The Tanzanian immigration officer who had given us student transit passes had validated them over a period of seven days. If we wanted to stay beyond this time, we had to obtain alternative papers. If not, we faced arrest and deportation again. During our first week in Kenya, we caught a bus to the UNHCR office in Nairobi. We requested refugee status and were both interviewed that same day.

The process of answering question after question about our circumstances and what we had experienced was exhausting. The UNHCR wanted to ensure we were genuine refugees in need of their protection in Kenya. Though we were as truthful as we could be, we also knew we couldn't admit we had lived in the UN refugee camp in Tanzania and had wilfully chosen to leave it. UN refugee laws dictated we could only claim refugee status in the first country we entered. After being interviewed, we were handed interim papers.

To our dismay, our initial request was denied. The reason given was that we had travelled through Tanzania first and were required to request refugee status there.

Then we remembered the piece of paper we had been given after our court hearing stating we had been ordered to leave Tanzania. Filing an appeal against the denials, this piece of paper eventually helped us gain the refugee status we needed. A mind-blowing realisation dawned on us – God had used our going to prison to help us stay in Kenya!

After we gained refugee status, we searched for a college that would help us finish our A-level education which had been interrupted by the war. When we were first told about Hope International School in Nairobi, which welcomed Burundian refugees, it was hard to believe such a school existed. We met the Dean of the school and explained our circumstances. Believing we had genuine cases, he signed us up to complete our last year of A levels free of charge. The course and exams would be conducted in French, the language Thierry and I had already studied in. This really was a dream come true. We had prayed much over the past few years that we could one day return to school. Seeing this prayer answered was a wonderful moment for both of us.

While we celebrated these small victories, the truth was Thierry and I still faced many hardships. We had run out of money and Jean was only able to provide us with the smallest financial support. He also let us share meals with his family, but some days when there wasn't much to go around, we went hungry.

One particular day, we were extremely hungry as we hadn't eaten well for several days.

'We can visit a church and see if they have meals for the poor,' Thierry suggested.

We knew of a large Pentecostal church that was a 45-minute walk away, so we decided to travel there. When we arrived, we were very disappointed. Though we were invited in to talk by the Bishop's secretary, after hearing about our situation, her response was to encourage us with words from the Bible and then pray with us. She then walked us to the door to see us off.

We left downcast and just as hungry as when we had first arrived. But even when we felt the church had let us down, God moved to show us he would never do the same.

Just moments later, we bumped into a man I recognised from a Methodist church gathering that Jean had invited us to.

He was walking in the opposite direction but turned back again when he realised he had seen us before.

'Hello, there!' he called out, striding up to us. 'How are you men? We have met before, I think?'

The man introduced himself as François Nitunga. Short and balding, he had a brilliant white smile and eyes that seemed to shine, I thought. He was carrying a brown paper bag that was filled with books.

'I am Theo and this is my friend, Thierry,' I said. 'I think we have seen you at a Methodist meeting.'

'Yes, yes,' François nodded, recalling the event. 'So where are you two off to today?'

'Nowhere, really,' I said. 'We are just walking back to Jean's house after a visit to the Pentecostal church.'

'You're walking? But it will take you a long time. Why don't you take the bus?'

'Oh, well, we have no money for the bus,' Thierry confessed. 'But it is okay, we are used to walking.'

François' expression was sympathetic when he heard Thierry's words. Bus fares were very cheap in Kenya so he must have realised we were very poor indeed.

'Oh, that is not good,' said François. 'I am sorry for you both.'

Reaching inside the brown paper bag, he brought out a handful of notes. He held them out to us.

'Here, take this. I want to help you a little.'

It was 2,500 Kenyan Shillings (about £20), a huge amount of money to us.

'Wow, this is very kind of you,' I said, not knowing how to respond. 'We cannot accept this.'

François' voice was full of warmth.

'It is no problem at all. Please keep it. God bless you and God provide for you both,' he said. 'Now, I must hurry on my way.'

Thierry's face was beaming as we watched François walk away.

He counted the notes in his hand again. 'Can you believe this?' he said. 'Our God is so good! He has given us food to eat today and for a few more days to come!'

Yes, our God was very good! We knew in our hearts that he would not abandon us. His provision that day was a clear reminder to us of this promise.

Before we knew it, two months had flown by.

We had been welcomed into Jean's neighbour's house on the condition that it was temporary. Now eight weeks had passed, we knew it was time to leave. Though we did not know where we would end up, we gathered our belongings into a few plastic bags.

We said goodbye to Jean and his family, and then we went on our way. Our plan was to take a walk and try to work out what we would do next. The money François had given us had run out by now. We only had a few shillings left in our pockets, just enough to buy a single loaf of bread perhaps.

We kept walking until we reached a neighbourhood that had a large community of Burundians. Feeling disheartened and tired from walking, we sat down on the pavement, watching as people passed by. We were sure we would have to spend the night outdoors and started discussing a few places we could do this comfortably. We weren't ready to think about the more serious problems we would soon face, such as our money running out and not being able to feed ourselves.

'Are we better off asking for a place back in a UN camp?' I asked Thierry. 'At least we will have food and shelter there . . .'

'Come on,' said Thierry. 'How can we go back to a camp? You know what life is like there. And we won't be able to study, either. Didn't we believe God brought us here to bless us? We just have to wait on him to help us.'

'I did believe that, too,' I told Thierry, 'but look at where we are now. We are homeless and will be starving soon. Perhaps God has taken everything away from us because he wants us to go back to the camp. Maybe he has a purpose for us there?'

Just as we were talking, we noticed someone had stopped right beside us.

We looked up to see a young man standing over us.

'Hi, there,' he said, addressing us in Kirundi. 'I'm sorry to disturb you. I just wanted to know if you boys were okay. Why are you sitting on the road?'

The stranger's expression reflected a genuine concern.

As we explained that we were homeless and trying to figure out what we should do, he didn't hesitate to respond.

'You must stay with me, then!' he said. 'Come and share what I have. If I eat, you'll eat, too. If I don't have any food, we will all not eat together . . .'

It was this incredible invitation that brought Félibien Ndintore into our lives. He was a Burundian student studying business in Kenya and he lived in a small, one-bedroom apartment with another student.

His act of kindness was one of the most astounding things I had ever experienced. Just seconds after we met and knowing nothing about us, Félibien had welcomed us into his home to live with him and share his food.

God had sent Félibien into our path in our hour of need. The most amazing thing was that Félibien and his housemate were Christians, too.

Though we would not understand this until much later, it was not just shelter and food that God wanted to bless us with through our meeting with him. God was working out a beautiful plan for our lives, even as we struggled to see a future for ourselves.

At Félibien's apartment, we were encouraged to make ourselves feel at home and given a place to sleep in the main living room. We met his flatmate, Léandre, who was studying Law at a university.

Thrilled to hear we were fellow believers, Félibien and Léandre told us about a church they attended every week called the Burundian and Rwandese Christian Fellowship. They met in a Pentecostal church building every Sunday afternoon and were predominantly made up of refugees like us who had fled the war. The first Sunday we joined them, we were surprised to discover we already knew the pastor. It was François Nitunga, the same man who had given us the generous donation when we couldn't afford to buy any food. We hadn't realised he was a pastor and it confirmed to us this church was a good place to be.

Excited, we offered to sing a worship song during the service – we had often sung together during our prayer meetings in the UN camp. The congregation greeted us warmly and made us feel at home. We were happy to meet so many other Burundian refugees – men and women who understood the heartbreak and troubles we had faced and were still facing daily.

There were about two hundred people at the service, which was conducted in Kirundi and even included a distribution of free maize flour for those who were struggling financially.

From that day onwards, we were regular attendants at the Fellowship.

Learning that we had led prayer meetings in the UN camp, François encouraged Thierry and me to become more involved in the services. Within a few months, we were invited to preach, too.

Joining the church was a pivotal moment in my life. Whereas before I wondered if God had a plan for my life, now I felt a growing sense of purpose.

Is this where God has brought me to serve? I thought to myself. *I can help my brothers and sisters who have suffered because of the war, just like I have. Is that why God allowed me to endure so much, so that I would be able to understand their pains and struggles?*

Though we were busy with our A-level studies each day, we made time during the evenings to help with the Fellowship's outreach and ministry to refugees. We visited the sick to pray for them and were invited to pray for those who were depressed or facing hardships. Among the refugee community, there were many issues Thierry and I could relate to. A few had been fortunate enough to find good jobs, but most struggled with poverty. Some were living on donations or sponsorship from charities such as the Roman Catholic Jesuits. Others had great difficulties finding work because even menial jobs would go to Kenyan nationals. Some refugees desperately missed home or the families they had become separated from with no means of knowing if they were still alive. Many had witnessed horrific events and were traumatised.

There was a great need within the community and I was convinced God had sent Thierry and I to help encourage and restore our people. We knew how great our God was and had experienced his miracles and abundant love. I felt compelled to share words of wisdom and hope from the Bible with them.

In turn, God seemed to confirm our calling by continuing to provide for us. Félibien and Léandre were students with little money to spare for extra meals and other provisions. But after joining the church, we received unexpected donations from several members of the congregation who could afford it. Understanding our difficult predicament, François also tried to give us something each month to help us buy food or pay for our travel while we ministered in people's houses. God's provision never failed to amaze us.

So I felt increasingly that Kenya was the place where God had called us to serve him. I was content there and finally had a sense of purpose. The only other thing I really desired was to begin my higher education and find a job to support myself. I also missed my family terribly and was eager to find out about their wellbeing. I wondered if God would give me the desires of my heart or if perhaps I was asking for too much. Once again, God's answer to prayer would not fail to astound me.

19

An Offer of a Lifetime

One Sunday at our fellowship service, a special guest arrived to preach and minister to us. His name was Canon Stanley Dakin. Born in England, 'Canon Stanley', as we called him, now lived in Nairobi and was the General Secretary of Church Army Africa (a large Anglican organisation). We listened to his sermon with enthusiasm, enjoying this *muzungu*'s (white man's) insight into the Word of God. That day, Thierry and I were also invited to sing together during worship.

After the service was over, Canon Stanley spent time meeting members of the congregation, shaking hands with people and asking them questions in Swahili. Approaching his 60s, with a head full of white hair, it struck me that he was a kind and compassionate man. His narrow eyes wrinkled as he smiled at those he met. Soon he came to greet Thierry and me, who were standing together.

'Your singing was very beautiful,' he told us. 'I really enjoyed it.'

'Thank you,' I said. 'It is a pleasure to sing for the Lord.'

'Yes, indeed,' he said, reaching inside a pocket of his trousers.

He handed us a small rectangular piece of card.

'This gives my contact details,' he said. 'Why don't you men visit me sometime?'

Thierry accepted the card and placed it inside his wallet. Canon Stanley smiled and bowed his head as he took his leave to greet some more people.

We were touched by his gesture. I hadn't noticed him give his card to anyone else. Even so, the truth was we were doubtful we would ever see the Canon again. Since we were poor refugees, and he was a foreigner, I was conscious that he might think we wanted something from him if we did go to visit him. We thought nothing of his offer again, forgetting Thierry had placed the card in his wallet.

Time passed and we continued to focus on our studies, while ministering to the refugee community in our free time. As the final exams of our A levels drew near, we stayed up well into the night, poring over our books and feeling a huge sense of gratitude that we had been allowed to study again. We sat our exams in July 1997 and were overjoyed when we passed and finally earned our A-level certificates. What a wonderful moment of achievement for us! We really thanked God for the opportunity he had given us.

Now that we had completed our A levels, I wondered what he had in store for us next.

I prayed earnestly that we might be able to go to university somehow and graduate. It was a struggle living on donations from members of our church and, being a man, it preyed on my self-esteem. I wanted to continue serving God in Kenya, but it was important that I support myself financially. I couldn't rely on handouts for the rest of my life. Surely God didn't want us to continue living in poverty?

Lord, take us out of this situation, I prayed. *Help us stand on our own two feet without having to rely on charity. We want to serve you here, but you have to make a way for us to become independent.*

I offered up this plea daily, believing that the God who had answered my prayers so many times before would do the same again.

It was startling when just the opposite began to happen.

The weeks after we had completed our A levels became the hardest period we had experienced yet. For the past seven months, we had received donations from members of the church who could afford to help us, even before we could express a need or lack. But now such gifts stopped without explanation. It was bizarre. François, who had been our biggest and most consistent supporter, also came to us with bad news. 'I will have nothing to give you for the next few months,' he told us regrettably. 'I am struggling myself. But take courage, I know the Lord will provide for us all. As soon as I have the funds again, I will give you what I can.'

Thierry and I felt overwhelmed. We were completely out of money and didn't know who to turn to for help. We could no longer afford the bus fares to visit members of our congregation so we could minister to them and pray. It felt like God had suddenly abandoned us and had stopped our ministry, too.

But why?

Believing it was just a temporary problem, we held onto hope. By now we were reliant on Félibien and Léandre to provide our meals each day, without contributing in any way as we had previously been able to. It felt humiliating but we hoped it was just for a short time.

But, as the weeks turned into months and nothing changed, Thierry and I started to panic. Why was God allowing us to go through this? Why had he stopped providing for us?

Before long, we had reached what felt like breaking point.

We were tired of having no money to feed ourselves. On top of this, it pained our hearts that we could no longer serve in the church the way we had before. As our self-esteem crumbled, we knew we had to discuss other options open to us. We could no longer bear to live the way we were.

'We could ask to be put in the UN camp in Kenya,' Thierry said. 'I think it's time we consider this a possibility.'

The camp was situated in the north of the country and I had heard the hot climate was difficult to bear.

'Perhaps returning to Mtabila might be better,' I suggested. 'Maybe the conditions have improved since we were last there. If we end up in a camp, isn't it wiser to return to one we are familiar with? The camp in Kenya might turn out to be worse.'

'This is just pointless,' Thierry sighed in resignation. 'Will it matter which camp we are in anyway? What will we be able to do in either of them? We will end up dying there. At the camp, every new day is just the same as the one before. It's a horrible way to live. Let's just head back to Burundi and try to make a future for ourselves. We know the university in Bujumbura is still operating. Perhaps, in time, we can enrol there. The Government will pay for us to study and get board so we won't have to worry about money.'

'But what about the war?' I said. 'There are no signs it will end . . . and aren't Hutu students still being targeted?'

'Well,' said Thierry, looking me squarely in the eyes, 'what other options do we have? Wouldn't you rather risk dying in the war, than staying here forever without a hope?'

We had heard several reports from Burundian refugees who had recently arrived from our country. The war had intensified between the Hutu rebels and the Government Army. Though in some areas of the country it was dangerous to be a young Hutu male, for you could easily be mistaken for a rebel or targeted in revenge for a rebel attack, in other areas the rebel stronghold meant that many Hutu families felt protected against attacks from the Army.

The risks involved in returning to Burundi were high, but Thierry's suggestion made sense to me. If we were lucky enough to return to our homes without encountering the Army, we could attempt to find a place at the university in Burundi's capital. There we could satisfy our burning desire to finish our education and find jobs. Then at least we would never have to live on handouts again. And if it happened that we died in Burundi as a result of our choice (we had learned there had been a massacre of Hutus at the university only months before), we would still be able to die with a sense of dignity we had been unable to find since we had left our own country.

'Okay,' I said finally, after I had considered his argument. 'Let's do it, then. Let's return to Burundi. If the Army kills us, so be it. We can't sustain our lives in Kenya any more.'

And so the decision to return to Burundi became firmly lodged in our minds.

But before we could go back, we faced one more challenge. We needed the funds to travel. Where would we find the money? Our plan was to visit the Burundian embassy in Kenya to tell them we wanted to go home. They would provide the documentation needed to clear any borders we had to pass. But we still needed the money to travel there.

As we tried to think of a way to raise some, I remembered someone who might be willing to help us.

'Canon Stanley!' I said to Thierry. 'We will go and visit him. Do you still have his card?'

'I don't understand,' said Thierry. 'Why do you want to see him?'

'Don't you see?' I explained. 'He is such a good and caring man. Maybe he will give us the money we need to go back. We will explain the hard situation we are in and tell him that our only hope of survival is if we return. I am sure he will help us.'

Thierry agreed it was a good idea. The truth was it was the only idea we had been able to come up with. I hated the thought of having to visit Canon Stanley to ask for the money we needed. After all, that is why we had avoided visiting him in the first place, in case he thought we wanted something from him. But now we weren't in a position to worry about what he would think of us. I knew it would feel demeaning to have to ask for money, but what other choice did we have?

Just a couple of days later, we travelled to the head office of Church Army Africa, where the Canon worked.

Approaching the reception area, we spoke to the lady behind the front desk.

'We have come to speak to Canon Stanley Dakin,' I said. 'If he is not too busy, we'd like to see him.'

I hoped the Canon would not be troubled by our unexpected visit.

The receptionist left her desk to peer into an office room. She quickly came out to usher us in.

'Yes,' she said. 'He can see you now.'

We followed her to the office door and stepped inside.

The Canon was looking over a document on his desk as we entered. He put it down immediately and stood up to greet us with a big smile.

'How wonderful to see you again,' he beamed. 'Welcome!'

He invited us to sit down at a large sofa to the side of his desk and came around to join us.

'Can I get you some tea or coffee?' he asked, reaching for the phone on his desk to make a call.

As we waited for our tea, Canon Stanley asked us how we were doing. He enquired after the church and asked about François and other church members, too.

We answered his questions politely and told him we were fine, too nervous to tell him why we had really come to see him.

After the tea and biscuits had arrived, as we were enjoying the refreshments, the Canon put his cup aside. He looked at us with a concerned smile and said: 'So, tell me, gentlemen, is there anything I can help you with?'

Thierry and I glanced nervously at each other.

After a moment of silence, I decided I would speak.

'I am sorry we didn't visit you before,' I said, 'and we didn't want to only visit you under these circumstances . . . but the truth is we are in a bad situation and we wondered if you might be the one who could help us.'

After I started speaking, the rest of the words seemed to tumble out. I explained how we had escaped the war in Burundi, run away from the Tanzanian refugee camp and had come to Kenya with only a few shillings left in our pockets. I explained that we had been living with Félibien and existing on donations we received, but now the money we had been receiving had dried up. Yes, we were grateful to God that he had allowed us to finish our A levels and had used us in the church to minister to our fellow refugees. But the situation had become so bad for us, we were at a critical point. We wanted to take the only opportunity we had to complete our studies and become independent working men. This meant returning to Burundi – we felt there were no other options.

'We have made our decision and now all we need is the money to return to Burundi,' I said. 'We know there is a chance we might lose our lives if we go back, but it feels like it is worth the risk if we can finish our education.'

The Canon had been listening intently as I spoke. He held his hands to his temples and appeared to be deep in thought.

Finally, he looked up and said: 'It is lunchtime now and you must be hungry. Why don't you both go to the canteen upstairs? Tell them I sent you there and eat whatever you want. When you come back, we can talk about this again.'

Thierry and I left the Canon's room not knowing how to feel. We weren't able to gauge how our request had been received. Did Canon Stanley want to help us? And if he did, what was he able to do for us? Did he believe we were genuine? I was convinced the Canon was a compassionate man. If he wasn't able to help us, I was sure no one else would.

Twenty minutes later, after we'd enjoyed a meal of sausage and chips, piled into our empty and nervous stomachs, we returned to his office.

'Sit down, boys,' he told us as we entered. 'I have been considering what you have asked me . . . Before I tell you what I think, though, let me ask you a few questions, if you wouldn't mind?'

'Of course,' Thierry said.

I nodded my consent, too: 'Yes, ask us anything.'

For the next ten minutes, Canon Stanley began to find out as much information as he could about our situation and the options we had.

How safe was Burundi at the current time?

Not very, we told him. Students were still being targeted by the Army. And yes, there had been a recent massacre at Bujumbura's university, but we hoped this meant it would be better prepared against further outbreaks of tension and violence.

What about Mtabila? Could we face returning there?

Life would certainly be tough in the camp and we couldn't guarantee conditions in Mtabila had improved. We would rather take a risk and go to Burundi.

Were we really willing to risk our lives just for the opportunity to study?

Our education and the chance to become independent was of utmost importance to us. Yes, we were willing to risk everything for these things, even our lives.

The Canon furrowed his wrinkled brow.

'Hmm . . .' He murmured and nodded as we talked. 'I see . . .'

Finally, when we had nothing left to say, his expression appeared to relax. He lifted his head and his smile reappeared.

'Gentlemen,' he said, 'my wife works for MAF – Mission Aviation Fellowship – which uses planes to fly all over East Africa. If you want, I can put you both on a carrier to Tanzania so you can return to the camp.' He paused then added: 'And if you really want to return to Burundi, I will provide you with the funds to get two flights there instead.'

I wanted to grab Thierry and dance him around the room.

'Thank you, Canon! Thank you so much!' I gushed. 'I can't tell you how grateful we . . .'

'Just a minute,' the Canon interrupted, holding up one hand. 'I haven't quite finished . . .'

Oh no! I thought. *What is it? Is there a catch?*

'There is a third option,' the Canon explained. 'And I want you to consider it, too.'

What he said next was beyond anything I could have imagined. He began to describe an opportunity that made me think I was dreaming – a dream in which some of my biggest hopes and desires were fulfilled, a dream which would transform my life forever. Except I wasn't dreaming. The Canon was really making us this offer.

'The third option is that I find both of you scholarships to train for ministry at Carlile College in Nairobi where the Reverend Tim Dakin, who happens to be my son, has been appointed by the board as Principal and could help,' he said. 'We will try to find you full board and accommodation and all your fees will be covered. At the end of three years, if you work hard enough, you could both graduate with an Advanced Diploma in Theology. What do you say, gentlemen?'

At first, we were stunned into silence. Then we couldn't contain our excitement . . .

'Yes! Yes!'

'Yes, we'd love to! Thank you!'

'Thank you! Thank you so much!'

'This is incredible!'

'Yes! Incredible!'

The joy I felt at that moment was indescribable. We had visited the Canon with a faint hope that he would help send us back to Burundi – where we would then grasp onto another small possibility of going back to school. We were already disillusioned and worn down, enough to think that our lives were headed nowhere and would never improve. But now God had opened the biggest door for us. Not only were we being offered the chance to complete our higher education safely in Kenya, without any cost to us whatsoever, but I felt convinced God had placed a special calling on our lives. If we had been successful enough to return to Burundi and enrol at the university, I would have chosen to study medicine. Thierry had wanted to study engineering. However, now we both jumped at the chance to study theology. It would set us up on a path to serve God not only in our free time, but with our careers, too. This unbelievable possibility of attending university in Kenya for free was certainly a gift from God and I was convinced he was telling us he wanted to use us.

That day in the Canon's office, the course of our future was changed forever. Within a week, the Canon had organised scholarships for us to Carlile College. Even though we were due to begin in August, he helped us to move into the dorm a month earlier as he knew we were struggling to feed ourselves. At the college, we now had three meals a day, our own rooms to sleep in and hot showers. God had amazed us once again by just how much he could do for us. And it wouldn't be long before we discovered the purpose behind so much he had allowed to happen.

Boarding at Carlile College felt like a dream to Thierry and I. Who could have imagined that life would change so dramatically for us? We were overwhelmed by how fortunate we were – how God had taken us from the refugee camp to such comfort. We would not have to worry about our meals or shelter for the next three years.

As our classes started, it was a greater joy to immerse ourselves in studying the Bible. We learned how to interpret God's Word and how to evangelise. I grew in my fervour to serve God. Mission was the word on my lips!

As we studied, Canon Stanley would often drop by the college. He took us out for a snack or drink whenever he had the opportunity. Always displaying an interest in the lives of the people he met, he asked us about our experiences in Burundi and Tanzania. One thing was apparent to me – God had graciously answered a lot of the persistent prayers I had offered up to him. Now here I was, safe in Kenya, and pursuing my higher education. There were just a few prayers that had been left unanswered. I missed my family desperately and yearned for information that would assure me they were doing well. But there was no way for me to contact them except if I returned to Burundi or the camp in Tanzania.

Then one day, during another visit from the Canon, he made us another generous offer as we sipped tea in a café. He wanted to send us back to Mtabila to search for our family and gather news about our loved ones. His wife would obtain permission for us to travel aboard one of MAF's planes.

We jumped at the chance to return.

This opportunity would help alleviate the constant worry that persisted in our minds. I hoped I could locate my brother Nixon and perhaps he would have information about the rest of my family.

It was December 1998 when we finally arrived back in Tanzania, more than two years since we had left the country.

Having obtained temporary travel documents from the Burundian embassy, since we held no passports, we flew on a tiny turboprop aircraft, with five other people. It was my first time flying and I felt like I was in a magical tin can. I gripped the handles of my seat in trepidation as the plane shuddered and roared into life and then finally swept up into the air. I was in awe as I watched the land shrink beneath me and thought about how I must be passing over the places where we had been arrested and held in jail, where we had spent our first months in Kenya and where we had ended up on the streets homeless. How minute those places seemed to be now and, in reality, how far behind us God had placed those disturbing times.

After landing in the town of Kasulu, we spent a night in a hostel before undertaking the 15-mile journey to Mtabila the next morning.

Returning to the camp was an overwhelming experience. I had left as a refugee but here I was returning as a visitor and student. I had run away illegally, with a conviction I never wanted to see the place again, but now my own free will had brought me back – and this time I would be allowed to leave the camp when I chose. How life had changed!

Obtaining permission to visit Mtabila wasn't simple. Thierry and I had no official reason to enter it, so we had to pay a bribe. This wasn't done in secret, however. We joined a queue of other refugees who were entering the camp without having gained permission to leave in the first place. They openly brought out money and placed it through the opening in the guard's hut to gain their entry, with no questions asked. As we cleared the iron bar and officer's hut that guarded the entrance, my senses took in the sights and sounds that had been so familiar to us just a few years back: the commotion and bustle of refugees going back and forth during their daily errands, the aroma of beans frying in palm oil or maize dough being baked on open fires outside shelters, and the dry red ground surrounded by forestland that was home to all of this activity. On first glance, the camp appeared to have changed in several ways. Now brick huts had been erected among the branch and twine shelters, although most still had corrugated iron sheets as their roofs. The condition of the road we walked on appeared better, too. The camp had also welcomed more refugees since we left as the increase in shelters was significant.

'Let us go back to our old place first,' Thierry suggested. 'I wonder what the boys will say when they see us!'

We had only been walking for five minutes when we were spotted by a couple of our old friends. It didn't take long before news spread that we had returned to the camp. As we continued, more and more of our former friends and neighbours joined our growing congregation, patting us on our backs and shaking our hands while firing a barrage of questions at us.

'Where have you been?'

'What happened to you two?'

'Do you have jobs now?'

'Why did you come back?'

We answered in simple statements, as best we could. There was so much to recount, we didn't know where to start.

Eliphaz was standing outside our old shelters when we finally reached them. Felix, Marc and several of the other boys were drawn outside by the commotion surrounding us. They were all amazed to see us. We hugged with huge smiles and hearty laughter.

'You have become *abazungu* (white men)!' they joked. 'Look at you both!'

'You have done well for yourselves!'

'Have you come to take us with you?'

There was a small tree outside our shelter and we sat under its shade as we began to talk and exchange information about the last few years of our lives. Thierry and I explained how we had escaped the camp and finally made it to Kenya after many tribulations. The boys were astonished to hear how God had allowed us to study with scholarships. In turn, they shared their news since we had departed.

Thierry learned his brother Muzima had left the camp to go to Mozambique where he had hoped to find work. They also told him they had heard reports his family were still in Burundi and living safely in a remote area that had been largely untouched by the war. As for life in the camp, the weekly prayer meetings were still being conducted in the shelter we had constructed for that purpose. Marc now led this prayer and singing ministry. He had become a full-time evangelist. Though some of the other boys had started small businesses to help support them, Felix and Eliphaz still remained inactive.

Conditions in Mtabila had not improved for many. It was true there were more services available now. The clinic had turned into a larger hospital and there were more primary schools operating, plus three secondary schools and even a law and nursing college that were governed by the camp. There were also opportunities to learn trades such as carpentry and handicrafts which NGOs offered to help refugees start their own businesses. A handful of refugees had made good money for themselves as a result of their businesses. But the reality was, the majority were still consumed with their day-to-day survival, with little hope for a future outside of the camp. No one knew when the war in Burundi would end and, if it did, if they would be able to return and regain the old lives they had lost. The boys also told us they were still being pressurised to join rebel groups and return to Burundi to fight.

After talking for nearly an hour, I felt eager to move on and see if I could find my brother Nixon. I left Thierry and told him I would be back in a short while. Taking the main road which headed towards my brother's shelter, I spotted an old neighbour from my hometown. When he saw me, he sprinted to reach me.

'Theo!' he said. 'Is that really you? You are here, too! You came back after so long!'

'Yes, yes, I am here to see everyone again,' I said, 'and it is good to see you, too! How are you?'

'I am well,' he replied. 'You must be so happy that you are going to see your mother and siblings today!'

His statement caught me off-guard.

'What do you mean?' I said. 'My mother and siblings? Have you seen them? Do you know where they are?'

'Oh yes,' he said. 'I thought you knew! I thought that was the reason you were walking this way. I have just seen them in the Transit Centre, right here in Mtabila. They just arrived from the camp in Nduta. They should be released very soon.'

I couldn't believe what I was hearing. Were my mother and siblings really in Mtabila? Had they really arrived the very same day as me?

Instead of continuing on my way to see Nixon, I took a different route to wait near the Transit Centre, a huge shelter that had been constructed to receive and register new refugees and to distribute supplies. A large part of me wondered if my friend's information was right. Was my family really going to walk out of the centre at any moment?

Less than half an hour later, just as he had reassured me, I saw my mother, surrounded by my brother and sisters, exiting the centre. I knew it was her as I recognised an old patterned *kitenge* (common African sarong) dress she was wearing, along with a bright scarf wrapped around her hair.

It was true. My family was really here in Mtabila!

I started towards them quickly, unable to contain my happiness. Mama saw me and the look on her face was unforgettable. Before I knew it, she was in my arms. We hugged and shook our heads in amazement at this unexpected reunion.

'Theo, you look so well!' my mother exclaimed. 'What has happened to you?'

'I will tell you everything later, Mama,' I said as I greeted my siblings who were with her. Didavine, Christine, Imelde, Onesime and Joyce were all there. It was incredible!

'Where is Normand?' I asked, realising he was missing.

'He is still in camp Nduta,' Christine told me. 'His wife just had a baby and they decided to stay.'

Our reunion that day was a magnificent one. A loving gift from God.

As the group of us arrived at Nixon's shelter, he looked like he had just seen a ghost. He wept tears of joy and disbelief at seeing us all together again. It was a tremendous reunion for all of us.

Soon we were all sitting outside on the ground, talking excitedly and sharing the events which had happened to us since we had been apart.

Mama looked pained as she informed me that Papa was still being held in jail. Just after his arrest, he had been transferred to a town a large distance away from their home. She had not been able to visit Papa and hadn't seen him for over two years. But she had received news that he was healthy and still awaiting his trial. She was certain he would be acquitted. She told me she had found some witnesses who had agreed to support his case and vouch that he had been one of the first to flee Burundi when President Ndadaye had been assassinated.

My mother also revealed that my family had left Burundi again just a few weeks prior to the Army increasing their attacks on Hutus in retaliation for a rebel attack. The violence looked as if it would reach their community, so they had been forced to hide out and sleep in vacant fields every night. After a few weeks, they decided to cross over to Tanzania. They had spent several days in the forest before a UN truck arrived to take them over to the Nduta camp, which was 55 miles away from Mtabila. Once there, they had requested a transfer to Mtabila as they wanted to locate Nixon. Previously, during their time in the forest, Normand's new wife had gone into labour and Mama had helped deliver her first grandchild. Weakened by childbirth, Normand's wife had chosen to stay in Nduta with her husband and new baby. But Mama and my remaining siblings had been moved to Mtabila a few days later.

It really was astounding that we had all arrived in Mtabila on the same day.

I was eager to hear how my brother Nixon had been doing. He shared how he had restarted his education in one of the secondary schools that was being run by the UNHCR. They had a syllabus and paid teachers, but no proper teaching aids like books or a blackboard. It was still a struggle for students to locate basic necessities such as notebooks or pens. I noticed that Nixon was wearing the same shirt and pair of trousers I had last seen him in. It saddened me to see how little his circumstances had changed since I had left.

Afterwards, I was grateful to share my testimony of what God had done for me since I had left the camp. Everyone agreed that God had answered my prayers in miraculous ways.

'God has blessed you so you could return and help us,' Mama said. 'Now you must try and help your father get out of prison.'

I gave my mother my word that I would do everything I could.

I couldn't have asked for a better gift than to see my family alive and well with my own eyes. I decided I would remain in Mtabila for a few more days to spend more time with them. Nixon welcomed us all into his shelter. During my stay, I was able to give my family some money that I had with me. I also bought them extra food provisions they were sure to need. How wonderful it felt to be able to aid them in this way.

Every night we were together, we met for daily prayer, just as we had during my childhood. We praised God for keeping us safe and bringing us all back together and we continued to pray that my father would remain in good health and be released soon. This was the last pressing prayer in my heart.

This time, leaving Mtabila was not a happy occasion. Saying goodbye to Mama and my siblings was difficult. I promised to return if I had another opportunity. Mama later told me that one of the biggest miracles she had ever witnessed was watching the MAF plane, carrying Thierry and me, fly over the camp – taking us back to Kenya where we would continue our education.

Little did we know, God would bring us to Mtabila again a few years later, this time with a different purpose.

While we studied at Carlile College and completed our diplomas, we also continued to attend the Burundian and Rwandese Christian Fellowship as we had done before. Through it, God's provision had returned to us. Shortly after we began our studies, the donations which had previously stopped began to come in again. As well as giving us some money to sustain us while we were at college, it meant we were able to continue our counselling and prayer ministry with our fellow refugees. I was very happy to return to the work I loved. It was during this time that a solid group of men dedicated to this refugee work began to emerge. As well as François and Félibien, it also included Frédéric Harerimana, the Assistant Pastor who had a special heart for refugees, Gervais Nyandwi, a compassionate and very prayerful elder, and Feston Manirakiza, another church leader who was known for his kind and loving personality. Our hearts were burdened by the plight of our brothers who were suffering so much as a result of the war. We knew they had little help available to them. Since God had done, and was still doing, much to restore me to a place of peace and contentment, I wanted them to know he could do the same for them, too. Thanks to my encounters with Tutsis such as Godance and Christine, and even with the Tanzanian woman who had helped us gain entry into Kenya, God had been working to chip away every residue of bitterness and anger that had built up in me since my childhood and as a consequence of what I had experienced in the previous years. And as I studied God's Word intensely, both privately and in our classes, I felt a greater release from these enslaving emotions. Pondering the work of Jesus on the cross, my past hatreds were put to shame, convincing me to forgive and allow my past wounds to heal. After all, wasn't this the purpose for which he came and suffered for us? I was challenged by the Word to forgive those whom I considered to be my enemies. As my process of healing continued, I felt eager to share my testimony with other refugees who were in need of the same restoration.

I believed God wanted to help them forgive those who had wronged them. They, too, could begin a journey of healing and reconciliation. For all of us, this process was sure to be a lengthy and difficult one, but I knew how freeing it was to obey God's call to forgive those who had hurt us.

As we persevered in praying together for our new ministry, it began to grow. We were able to distribute more food and assistance to those in need and we partnered with other churches to help combat the growing cases of HIV/AIDS infections that were increasing among the refugees as a result of promiscuity, an unhealthy distraction from the idleness, poverty and hopelessness they faced. I was very happy to be part of this work in Nairobi. It was fulfilling to help my own people with such issues.

Time passed and, before we knew it, we had reached the final term of our course. At this point, I was very excited about the future that lay in store for me. I had been surprised by an offer to join an Anglian Church in Nairobi as an evangelist after I graduated, and the salary would be good. It was a dream role. I would be doing work that I loved and I would still be able to continue the refugee ministry I was part of in my spare time. On top of that, I would finally be a financially independent man. I hoped to send money back to the camp in Mtabila to help my family there. Thierry had also been offered a similar role in another church. As the weeks passed, we prayed daily that God would guide us and give us wisdom with our future choices.

But as I began to pray, something very troubling began to happen.

Every time I remembered my family, friends and other Burundians still living in the refugee camps, I prayed that God would use his church as a solution to the many problems and difficulties they faced. But each time I did, I was sure I heard a clear voice saying something to my spirit: *'You are the church!'*

I am the church? What do you mean by this, Lord? I prayed. *Is that you speaking? I don't think I understand. Yes, I am part of your church, but what are you saying?*

My confusion made me devote myself to prayer even more. As I tried to discover what God was saying, I realised a new thought was forming in my mind. It was one, in my own reasoning, that made no sense and was really the last thing I wanted to do. Yet the thought kept returning to me each time I prayed.

Go back to the camps in Tanzania! Help your people!

Go back? To the refugee camps? Was this really God speaking to me?

Alarmed by what I sensed I was hearing, I decided to tell Thierry about my inner conflict.

He listened carefully as I told him the exact words I felt God had been speaking to me.

'Why would God be asking me to go back to the refugee camps?' I said. 'I have just been offered a wonderful job in Nairobi and I am happy doing ministry here. God did so much to bring us out of Tanzania, I don't think I could bear to go back again. Do you think I'm hearing right, Thierry?'

Thierry always had a sensible approach to life and I was certain he would have some great advice for me. I imagined he would tell me I was mistaken – that my thoughts were probably a result of the guilt I felt because I had left the camp while those I loved still remained there. I was sure he would also insist that God wanted to use me in Kenya and there would be no point in going back to a place where I'd face too many overwhelming problems.

But as I watched Thierry's face, I saw that he was hesitating to speak.

'Hey! What's the matter?' I asked Thierry. 'Are you okay? Why are you so quiet?'

Thierry placed a gentle hand on my shoulder and took a deep breath.

'You asked me if I thought you were hearing right.' he said. 'Well . . . I think it is God speaking to you and you need to listen.' He paused and then added: 'You see . . . God has been telling me the same thing, too.'

20

An Amazing Door

I had no idea God had been speaking to Thierry, too – telling him he also needed to minister in the Tanzanian camps. However, it was the last thing I wanted to hear.

Living in the refugee camp had been a traumatic ordeal for me. Being among thousands of people who were displaced, hopeless and suffering, was naturally very distressing. We had too many painful memories from our time there.

Then there was the issue of feeling confined, especially since camp restrictions had tightened. Gaining our sense of freedom in Kenya, where we had been able to live as we chose and strive towards the futures we had dreamed of, had been an invaluable gift. We no longer faced contempt and disrespect from Tanzanian citizens and authorities, and we finally had a chance to regain our self-worth. But here was God telling us to go back to the camps in Tanzania, just as everyone there wished they could leave.

What, then, were God's plans for us? Would we be able to serve him in a place we were loath to return to?

However much we wished to find excuses as to why we couldn't go back, we couldn't shake off the conviction this was what God wanted.

'Let's speak to François,' Thierry suggested that same day. 'He might give us some guidance on what to do next.'

It was hard to miss the excitement on François' face when we told him what we believed God was saying to us. François had been visiting several camps in Tanzania and he was eager to send workers there to minister to the vast needs he saw.

'Since you have come from a Tanzanian camp and understand how they operate,' he said, 'I believe you'd be the perfect men for the task. If you feel this is what God is saying, then my advice is to trust and obey him. I will help make this possible and mobilise as much support for you as I can find.'

I looked over to Thierry, who was shaking his head in wonder.

God was making his intentions for us very clear. Now our pastor had agreed it was a good idea and had promised to help our efforts, could we resist what God was telling us to do?

Later that day, I sat on the edge of Thierry's dorm bed as I voiced my concerns to him: 'I can't believe I have to turn down my job offer in Nairobi. I know I want to serve God, but this seems too difficult. If we are to return to the camps, how will we provide for ourselves? We will have no income.'

There were other obstacles in our way, too. To work in Tanzania, we would need passports so we could enter and work there legally. Yet there was no way we could get these without returning to Burundi first, and that wasn't an option. On top of everything, we were required to have a local employer so that a work permit could be issued to us.

'Theo,' Thierry said, 'I have no idea how we are going to get all of these things and make this happen. But you have to relax. If it is God's will, let's just pray about it. If God wants us to go to Tanzania and work in the camps, let's see if he can make these things possible.'

'So what are you saying, Thierry?' I asked. 'That we just wait and see what happens?'

'Exactly,' said Thierry. 'Let's do what we can, and then let's see if God will do the rest. If he does, then we'll know for sure this is what he wants us to do.'

I liked the sound of Thierry's idea. I knew that among the difficulties we could face in Tanzania, the hardest part for me would be returning to a state of poverty. If God wanted me to work in the refugee camps, I wanted a stable income, especially after I had worked so hard to gain my diploma and independence. I was also sure it would be near impossible for us to acquire passports. If God managed to get us the things we needed and were asking for, I knew I would be ready to go back and do the work it seemed he was urging us to do.

Thierry and I began praying that God would meet our requirements. As we did, Thierry had the idea of contacting a friend of his called Sylvia, who also happened to be a Burundian MP. He had met her several months back when her son, who was studying in Nairobi, had fallen into an unhealthy lifestyle. Thierry had befriended him and been able to minister to him. This led to him giving his life to Jesus and changing his ways. After hearing her son's testimony, Sylvia herself had become a Christian. Because of this, Thierry and Sylvia had formed a close bond and would meet when she came from Bujumbura to Nairobi every two months to visit her son.

'I will do what I can to help you, but I can't promise anything,' Sylvia told Thierry when he saw her next.

But then, just eight weeks later, Thierry received a phone call at the college.

'I'm back in Nairobi,' Sylvia said. 'Come and see me to collect your passports.'

We were stunned.

Here we were, never having left Kenya or even filled out passport application forms, and we suddenly had our very first passports in our hands. Sylvia had taken our passport photos along with her, but that had been it. What should have been an impossible task had required no effort at all from us. God had made a way!

Meanwhile, François was eager to help find funds for our work in Tanzania and for our salaries. He spoke to the Reverend Canon Doctor David Williams who had become the Principal of Carlile College during our second year. Dr Williams was excited about the prospect of sending two of his graduates into the refugee camps. After discussing the possibilities with François, he picked up the phone straight away and called some of his contacts in the United Kingdom. Before long, we received more good news. St Mary's Anglican Church in Thame, England, and the UK charity, Barnabas Fund, had agreed to jointly sponsor Thierry and myself to go to Tanzania. Now we would have salaries for the work we were to do. God had provided the desire of my heart.

The only thing we needed now was a local agency to employ us. Once again François and Dr Williams set to work to find contacts in Tanzania.

One day, we were summoned to the Principal's office.

'Gentlemen, guess what?' said Dr Williams enthusiastically. 'You won't have to wait much longer to go to Tanzania. I have spoken to a church leader in Kagera. He wants to welcome you both to work with his church in the refugee camp in Lukole. It is all arranged!'

It was marvellous news.

Returning to Tanzania, and especially to a refugee camp, had initially seemed like a nightmare. But as I listened to Dr Williams's words, I couldn't help but feel a rush of excitement. God had given us everything we needed to return. He had shown us he was with us and had a wonderful plan for us. I was so amazed by his works and blessings in our lives, I knew I wanted to serve him wherever he wanted to take me. If this meant returning to the refugee camps, I finally felt ready to accept this. At least I would go knowing that my ever-loving and faithful Father would be with me.

Since we had graduated with our Higher Diplomas in Theology two months earlier, and not wanting to waste any time, we prepared to leave Kenya just one week after Dr Williams's news. We boarded a bus from Nairobi to Mwanza in Tanzania, where we would be travelling onwards to Kagera to meet a church leader called Reverend Ruhinga and start our work in the Lukole refugee camp. As we began the journey, staring out of the window as the landscape of Kenya passed us by, we felt bolstered with hope and confidence. We had a comforting knowledge that we were in God's will, doing what he wanted us to do. He wanted to use us to serve Burundian refugees in Tanzania and it would be an honour to do his work. For the first time I could remember, my future felt significant and purposeful. What could go wrong now?

We arrived at the border of Tanzania at 6 a.m. the next day. This time, we were able to purchase visas from the border. We handed over our passports without any questions from the immigration authorities.

We boarded our bus again, reached Kagera by the afternoon, and then left the following morning to meet Reverend Ruhinga at his office. Although we hadn't told him we were coming, we had been assured he was expecting us at some point.

The building we arrived at was a modest brick bungalow which had been built on top of a hill in the small town. It was a sunny day and the view from the hill was beautiful. Pretty green savannahs stretched out before us in every direction.

'This is going to be a regular sight for us from now on,' I said to Thierry, feeing thrilled. 'Can you believe it? Isn't the view magnificent?'

An assistant answered the door to us.

'Yes?' he said. 'Can I help you?'

'We have come to see the Reverend Ruhinga,' I said. 'Is he available?'

We were taken to his office.

Reverend Ruhinga sat behind a desk and welcomed us in with a friendly smile.

'Please take a seat,' he said, 'and then you can tell me what I can do for you.'

'We are the men who have been sent by Dr Williams in Nairobi,' I said. 'We know he has spoken to you about us already. We only arrived here yesterday but we are very eager to begin our work with you in the Lukole camp.'

The Reverend frowned. He looked confused.

I was holding a letter in my hand, one Dr Williams had written to him introducing us and referring back to their earlier talks about the work we desired to do. It also requested that he apply for our work permits as soon as he was able to.

I gave the letter to the Reverend. I was sure he was used to dealing with new and different projects every day. This would help clarify things.

But as he read the letter, Reverend Ruhinga appeared agitated.

'Ai,' he muttered as he came to the end. 'What is this about?'

Thierry looked at me, perplexed. This wasn't the reaction we had been expecting.

'Is there a problem?' I asked anxiously. 'Do you need some more information?'

'Oh . . . no, no . . .' the Reverend said. 'Just give me a few minutes. I will just speak to my assistant for a moment, if you'll excuse me.'

He left the room and closed the door behind him.

Thierry and I were both concerned now.

What was going on? Reverend Ruhinga seemed upset about something.

Fifteen minutes must have passed before he finally returned. He walked back into the room and sat behind his desk again.

Clearing his throat, the Reverend looked at us plainly.

'I am very sorry, but there must have been some confusion,' he said, 'because I am not sure we are ready to do this at the moment. To be honest, I hadn't been expecting you so soon . . .'

Our hopes deflated.

'But let me see what we can do,' he continued. 'We have no place for you to stay here, but I think I can arrange accommodation if you are able to pay $300 [£230] each, every month. As for the work permits you need, this will be more problematic for me. I cannot promise my help.'

The disappointment was painful. We hadn't been prepared for this. There was no way we could afford $300 per month. Even if we could, if the Reverend couldn't help us gain our work permits, there was no way we could stay in Tanzania.

'We will think about your kind offer,' Thierry said politely, standing up to leave.

We bowed respectfully and then we made our way outside.

We were crushed.

What were we going to do now? The door to our work with Reverend Ruhinga had been firmly closed. But why?

'Thierry, we have little option now,' I sighed, as we walked down the hill, away from the Reverend's office. 'The only thing we can do is go back to Kenya. Maybe this was not what God was telling us to do.'

'Theo!' Thierry said. 'Don't think like that. You know God showed us this was his will. We'll just have to find someone else to work with.'

'But how?' I said. 'We don't know anyone else who can help us enter the camps and get our work permits.'

'Just a minute!' said Thierry, halting suddenly. 'Actually, I have just had an idea . . . maybe I do know someone . . .'

'You do?' I said. 'Who?'

'Well,' said Thierry. 'I cannot guarantee he will give us the things we need, but perhaps he will do what he can for us . . .'

Thierry explained he had heard of a Burundian man named Hezroni Ntizompeba who had dedicated himself to the cause of our refugees in Tanzania. A pastor from our fellowship had spoken very highly of him, describing him as a sincere man of God. Despite being offered other work opportunities, Hezroni had chosen to stay in several of the refugee camps so he could carry out the work he was passionate about. At present, he was involved in projects operating in several camps.

Thierry also knew that Hezroni now lived in a town called Tabora, which was more than 200 miles away from Kagera. Thierry seemed convinced that it was a trip worth making.

Our plans altered, we enquired about the bus routes to Tabora. Soon we were on a two-day journey to meet a stranger who we hoped could help us.

After the carefree excitement we had enjoyed just a few hours back, before meeting Reverend Ruhinga, the setback we faced was hard to stomach. I didn't want to get my hopes up about what Hezroni could do for us. It was better not to expect anything.

At this point in my life, I knew God was able to move mountains on our behalf if that was his will for us. But I was confused about why our plans with Reverend Ruhinga hadn't worked out, especially after everything God had done to get us to Tanzania. It didn't make sense. What was God doing?

God, if you want us to stay in Tanzania, you have to open another door for us. We really don't know what you are trying to tell us.

After two days of travelling, we reached Tabora. We were two very tired and apprehensive men. Since we had never met Hezroni before, we really didn't know what to expect. Even if the good things we heard about him were true, was there anything he could really do for us? Perhaps the most we should expect was advice on what to do next.

Locating Hezroni's home was an easy task. We were directed to his brick compound by the first person we asked.

Knocking on his front door, we had no idea what would await us.

It was Hezroni's wife who opened the door, a tall woman with a gentle, kind face.

'Are you here to see my husband?' she asked, stepping back to let us in. 'Please come inside!' She reached over to take our bags from us and put them aside.

Just seconds later, Hezroni appeared.

The first thing that struck me about him was his dazzling toothy grin. Though we were two strangers he had never met before, and he had no idea why we had come, he seemed unusually excited to see us.

Shaking our hands energetically, he asked us an unexpected question before we could even introduce ourselves. He said: 'Before we talk, can we just thank the Lord that you are here?'

'Of course,' we both replied at once, feeling a little bewildered.

Standing in the same spot, he closed his eyes and bowed his head in prayer.

'Loving Father,' he prayed, 'I thank you for sending these two young gentlemen to visit us today. I know you have a purpose for all things. Bless us as we meet today. In Jesus' name we pray!'

Hezroni's prayer warmed my heart. It was one of the nicest welcomes I had ever had. I hoped it was a positive sign.

'It is good to have you here,' Hezroni said, urging us to sit down. 'Do tell me if I can do anything for you.'

'Well,' Thierry began, 'we have come here because we have nowhere else to go . . . And we wondered if you might be the person to help with a situation we are in . . .'

Thierry explained how we had come to Tanzania because of God's clear direction to serve the Burundian refugees in the camps. We had come believing we would have an employer here, though we had just discovered this was not the case. Now we were reluctant to go back to Kenya without seeing if God would open another door for us. Was Hezroni able to help us?

As Hezroni listened keenly to Thierry's words, I wondered what he would say. Would he know of an employer who could help us gain access to the refugee camps? Would he be able to employ us himself?

After listening to our story and understanding what we needed, Hezroni astounded us with his response.

He said: 'So long as you have one vision – that of reaching out to our fellow Burundian refugees – and so long as you are servants of God, I am taking your visit as a gift from God. Please be welcomed into our home and stay with us. I will help you in whatever capacity I can.'

I was truly overwhelmed by Hezroni's pledge to us. It was such a generous and trusting response.

And it would prove to be the answer to our predicament.

Surely God's hand has led us here! I thought.

Before I had a chance to thank him, Hezroni stood up again. This time, he lifted his hands heavenwards to pray: 'God, you have heard what we have discussed. Be with us now and help us to do your will.'

It was another earnest prayer that warmed our hearts.

After he finished praying, Hezroni's wife appeared to show us to their guest room, inviting us to store our bags inside and then wash ourselves with the buckets of warm water she had prepared for us.

'Is this really happening to us?' I said to Thierry as we unpacked our clothes. 'Isn't God so wonderful?'

Thierry chuckled.

'Perhaps we should know that by now,' he said. 'How could we have doubted he would show us the way?'

I really was in awe of everything that was happening to us. God had given us an opportunity to stay in Tanzania and worked out another way for us to minister in the refugee camps.

The next day, we discovered the real extent of the opportunity God had opened for us. We learned that Hezroni had established his ministry with refugees within 11 different camps in Tanzania, including some of the older settlements dating from 1972. He told us he was happy to have us join the work he was doing.

We soon realised why God had closed the door to us working with Reverend Ruhinga and his church.

Now, it wasn't just one camp we had access to, but several! And where we might have been restricted to working with one denomination in the camp in Lukole, Hezroni had built ties with multiple denominations. God had made a way for us to work with all churches in the camps!

Though we were strangers to him, Hezroni took us at our word and welcomed us to live with him for as long as we needed to. Within a month, he had arranged for our permits to arrive and we began our work.

This amazing door was the one God had intended to open for us all along.

21

The Promise Fulfilled

Over the next two years, Thierry and I made our home within several of the refugee camps in Tanzania, in what was to be an itinerant ministry for us. I felt like Nehemiah returning to Jerusalem after its destruction. It was hard not to be overwhelmed by the hardships the refugees faced every day. Their pain and suffering seemed relentless.

The majority of refugees had turned their hand to cultivating the land on the plots they had been given. But this was never enough to support them beyond what they were eating every day.

Only a minority succeeded with small business endeavours. Those who undertook illegal measures to smuggle in highly desired goods appeared to prosper the most. Some even purchased cars for themselves.

While schools had been organised to provide primary and secondary education for children, they were poorly equipped and often packed to capacity. In addition, there was rarely anything beyond secondary education available.

Certain NGOs offered scholarships for capable students to study outside the camps, but those who benefited were just a handful out of tens of thousands. Others who were eager to continue their education or find work simply ran away from the camps just as we had. There were both good and bad reports concerning the success of their efforts.

Crime within the camps was on the increase because of black market and political activities, with the cover of night making a great breeding ground for both. Tensions and conflict between those who supported different political groups became another source of trouble.

All the while, the refugee population within the camps continued to swell. Couples favoured having large families as it meant they would be given more food and supplies since children's rations were still the same as adult ones. There was no foresight concerning how these big families might sustain themselves if and when a return to Burundi was made possible.

There was also a range of health issues that affected many refugees. Promiscuity in the camp had led to a huge epidemic of HIV/AIDS. With a lack of education and services available, those infected were often stigmatised and suffered seclusion and rejection by the rest of the community. Their health would decline fast under camp conditions.

Disillusioned youngsters, unable to study and with little else to do, turned to drugs and homemade alcohol. Along with the physical health problems these caused, they battled the despair they felt, too. They were lost and distressed, with no hope for a future they once believed they could have.

The Christian churches that served the refugees were also having issues of their own. Some preachers led their congregation to believe the camp was the desert wilderness, where God was testing his people. Others encouraged a confused notion of the kingdom of God where Burundi was described as the very kingdom itself. If you died in the camp and never returned 'home', it meant you had not reached heaven.

Under Hezroni's leadership, Thierry and I focused on two main projects on our return to the camps. Firstly, we addressed the issue of the HIV epidemic since it was a growing problem, with little available to curb its spread and consequences. We educated refugees about safe sex practices and encouraged churches to be involved in stopping its spread. We instigated the growth of care programmes to deal with those who had contracted the disease, discouraging stigmatisation and preaching Jesus' mandate to 'love each other as I have loved you' (John 15:12). Prior to this, it had been common practice to excommunicate those who had contracted the disease.

Our next priority was to train pastors about the Bible: how to read and interpret it correctly and how to help congregations in the camp apply it to their lives. This included teaching refugees how to love their neighbours in the camp, encouraging them to confess their sins, especially in relation to any war crimes that had been committed, and encouraging them to reach a place where they could forgive those who had hurt or killed their families and friends.

It was a wonderful ministry to be part of. Though it was a challenge returning to camp conditions and was often taxing on our spirits, we poured our hearts and souls into serving our brothers and sisters, just as we believed God wanted us to.

During our time in this ministry, it was another blessing that I was able to return to Mtabila on numerous occasions as we also operated our projects there. I stayed in a shelter with my mother and siblings and relished every opportunity to spend time with them. Because of the money I was earning, I was able to help support them and their quality of life improved greatly.

In 2002, after two years of working in the refugee camps, God opened up another incredible door. This was an opportunity for me to complete a BA degree in Biblical and Intercultural Studies at All Nations Christian College in Hertfordshire, England.

It was June 2004 when I finally completed this two-year course and returned to Kenya to begin teaching at Carlile College. During this time, I also returned to the refugee work that was still being carried out through the Burundian and Rwandese Fellowship. In 2003, it had been shaped into an official NGO called Rema Ministries. 'Rema' is a Kirundi word which means 'take courage'. Ever committed to our work with refugees, Thierry, François, Félibien, Gervais, Frédéric, Feston and I, had formed this organisation to care for the needs of our fellow Burundian refugees. Through Rema Ministries, we were able to dedicate ourselves to addressing a wide range of issues we had never handled before. Not only did we continue our HIV/ AIDS work and training church leaders, we also focused on the issues surrounding reintegration once the refugees started to return to Burundi after peace deals to end the war were signed in 2000.

Ten per cent of Burundi's population were waiting to return, but they faced huge obstacles. Often the land they had abandoned had been taken over by strangers and there were no laws in place to help them regain it. They had no financial means to start their lives again through rebuilding their homes or purchasing new areas of land to farm. The country's economy was struggling and there were limited jobs available.

In addition, the younger generation lacked education and were used to surviving on a relief system. They possessed no skills except a limited knowledge of how to cultivate land. Some even spoke Swahili better than they did Kirundi or French. The majority were accustomed to life in the camp. In the older camps which had been set up before 1993, the generation that had been born there had no affection for a country they did not know. Instead they identified themselves with the camp, though they still fought a culture which did not allow them to be absorbed into the Tanzanian community.

On another level, there were still boiling issues of reconciliation to be addressed. There were many wounds that had never healed, even after years in the camp. When Hutus repatriated to areas where they had Tutsi neighbours, these feelings were breeding grounds for hostile communities. This meant that re-integration with their Tutsi brothers was also vital.

Rema Ministries became involved in the following areas: offering returnees free healthcare, teaching income-generating skills (e.g. education about loans and how to save money), peace-building initiatives such as trauma healing and community dialogue processes, and also research-based advocacy to help us address the Burundian Government on behalf of Burundian refugees (and even for the Congolese and Rwandan refugees who had fled to Burundi because of their own conflicts). It was our desire that Rema Ministries cared for the welfare, needs, burdens and rights of those who had become refugees as a result of Burundi's civil war.

Looking back over my life and everything I had been through, how could I deny that God had listened to and answered my prayers for help and blessing? Above all, because of his grace, he had honoured my desire to serve him with my life. I had seen him transform every difficult and painful experience I had been through into an opportunity to use it for good. For he sent me to those who were suffering, traumatised, bereaved, bitter, angry, impoverished, broken, displaced, anguished, disenchanted and hopeless, just as I had been. But God had done so much for me, and within me, compelling me to bring his message of hope and peace to those whose pain I understood well. I craved to see them restored through the mercy, goodness and love of God, in the same way that I had been restored. And because of his abundant grace, I learned how the ability to give and receive forgiveness was a vital step towards the destination of wholeness that God intends for all his beloved children.

I give God the glory for every good thing he has done in my life and continues to do in the lives of the refugees I encounter every day.

Psalm 71:19–24

Your righteousness, God, reaches to the heavens,
    you who have done great things.
    Who is like you, God?
Though you have made me see troubles,
    many and bitter,
    you will restore my life again;
from the depths of the earth
    you will again bring me up.
You will increase my honour
    and comfort me once more.
I will praise you with the harp
    for your faithfulness, my God;
I will sing praise to you with the lyre,
    Holy One of Israel.

My lips will shout for joy
  when I sing praise to you –
  I whom you have delivered.
My tongue will tell of your righteous acts
  all day long,
for those who wanted to harm me
  have been put to shame and confusion.

Epilogue

In August 2004, I married my wonderful wife, Christine, having met her through her sister who attended the Burundian and Rwandese Fellowship in Nairobi. My marriage to her was proof of the healing God had allowed in my life, since Christine's mother is a Tutsi. Our union has brought many Tutsis into my life, whom I love and consider dear to me. Not just as friends now, but as family members. We have also been blessed with four beautiful children, Précise (born in 2005), Prévoyant (born in 2006) and twins Kerry Princia and Danny Prince (born in 2010).

My family finally left Kenya and returned to live in Burundi's capital, Bujumbura, in 2008, since Rema Ministries' work began to focus on aiding the returnees to the country. It wasn't an easy event for me. I met many people who had been involved in serious war crimes against Hutus, or who had been implicated in the murders of my family members and friends. I had to deal with issues of forgiveness again, as well as being able to reintegrate back into the Burundian community. But God was able to continue his work within me. Others, such as my aunt, who had lost four children when they were barricaded into a hut and burned alive, tells me she will never be able to forgive those horrific crimes. She is deeply traumatised by the event, still reliving the horror of that day in recurring night-mares. The act of forgiveness is sometimes extremely difficult. Often there needs to be a deep releasing of pain at the cross before the process of forgiveness can begin and true healing occur.

On my return to Burundi, I also reunited with people I thought I would never see again because of the war. This included some of the Christian Union friends I had fled the country with back in 1993. I was amazed to learn that God had protected us all through the war: Jean Claude and Jean Prime had remained in Burundi after we had departed from each other but Gelte, Philipe and David had made it safely to different Tanzanian camps.

My father was eventually released from prison in 2001, after spending nearly six years there. He was acquitted in a trial accusing him of multiple murders that had been committed during the war. After his release, my father left for Tanzania and eventually joined my mother and siblings in the camp in Mtabila. Sylvia, the MP friend Thierry had made in Tanzania, played a huge role in his release. In 2004, Papa, Mama and the rest of my siblings left the camp and returned to Burundi to resettle on a new piece of land in the southern part of the country. Today, my father continues to cultivate his land and remains active in the field of local politics. He was able to forgive those who put him in prison. My mother continues to be the sweet, loving and prayerful soul that she is. As for my siblings, Normand became a builder, Nixon is a judge in the Appeal Court and Christine is a teacher. Didavine, Imelde, Onesime and Joyce are all involved in completing different levels of education, trying to make up for what was missed during the war and their time in the refugee camp.

Having been integral in the start of Rema Ministries, Thierry left the organisation in 2005 to become a pastor in the Anglican church of Burundi. He also became a theology lecturer at a local university. We remain very close friends to this day.

Rema Ministries has established itself as a peace-building organisation committed to the rights of people in forced displacement situations, particularly refugees, the internally displaced and returnees. I continue to work there in my current role as Director.

As for the condition of our country, as we stand in 2017, there are still troubling instabilities in Burundi.

In August 2000, under pressure from the international community, peace deals were signed between the Government and several important political parties in Burundi, although it wasn't until November 2003 that there was a major shift in security, when the largest Hutu rebel group, the CNDD-FDD (National Council for the Defence of Democracy – Forces for the Defence of Democracy), declared a ceasefire. The peace accord, known as the Arusha Peace and Reconciliation Agreement, finally ended Burundi's civil war and what was nearly ten years of conflict.

Government and CNDD-FDD representatives agreed to share power for two years until a General Election was held. President Pierre Nkurunziza, a Hutu and former head of the CNDD-FDD, was sworn in as President of Burundi in August 2005. In 2005, the Arusha Peace and Reconciliation Agreement was also translated into the Burundian constitution. Even then, it would take another four years before all remaining rebel groups finally laid down their arms.

Burundi experienced a period of peace until 2015, when Pierre Nkurunziza opted to run for a third term as President. Although the Arusha Peace and Reconciliation Agreement clearly defined a limit of two presidential terms, the Constitutional court supported an argument that his first term did not count since he was elected by parliament, not by the electorate. A significant number of people were unhappy with this result, believing the judges had delivered their ruling under unfair pressure.

President Nkurunziza's actions sparked demonstrations against what people said was his abuse of the Arusha Peace and Reconciliation Agreement. Some demonstrations turned violent. Then on 13 May 2015, there was a failed coup against the President. This resulted in a Government effort to regain control through the silencing of some of the media and what some claimed was excessive power used against opposition and civilians, including arbitrary detention, torture and assassinations.

On 24 July 2015, President Nkurunziza was elected to a third term, to run for the next five years. Part of his opposition armed themselves and engaged the Government in a low-scale war in some neighbourhoods in the capital, Bujumbura. This led to many deaths (estimated at more than 800) and a reported 250,000 Burundians fleeing the country. The President refused to welcome peacekeeping troops to help diffuse the crisis.

Since then, tensions in Burundi remain high. There have been reports, contested by the Government, of extrajudicial killings, unexplained disappearances and torture carried out by security forces and the ruling party's youth league against perceived opponents.

As is evident by the most recent disturbances, Burundi's deep hurts and tensions could take decades and even centuries to heal. And they carry the potential to make violence and war erupt easily.

Of course, our country still suffers from the effects of trauma and brokenness caused by the 1993 war – and the wars and conflicts before it. Part of the 2000 peace accord sought the set-up of a Truth and Reconciliation Commission to examine war crimes. It would uncover the truth about these crimes and attempt to reconcile those involved. An additional arm that could make prosecutions, if needed, was also desired. The Commission became a reality in 2014, though it has faced many challenges, the most recent being the disturbance caused by the 2015 political crisis. The mandate it holds currently seems impossible because of the latest political unrest and economic hardships which have followed as a result.

We must remember to ask our Almighty Father – who hears and is able to answer prayer – to continue to heal our land, reconciling and restoring the hearts of every Burundian affected by conflicts of the past and in the present. Pray with me that Burundi will have good leaders, with the wisdom and integrity to bring our country out of its current difficulties. And pray with me that Burundi will soon encounter a new and lasting period of peace.

Acknowledgments

I can't thank Theo Mbazumutima enough for sharing his incredible testimony with me and dedicating much time and effort to painstakingly recall the events in his life, even the smallest details of his often traumatic experiences. You told me your story with the most stunning humility and honesty. I often struggled to hold back tears as you shared your journey, and it still remains a source of encouragement to me. I will forever be in awe of how you traded your deep sorrow, pain and trauma for joy, peace and hope – allowing our Loving Father to use you as a testimony and blessing to your fellow Burundians and other refugees.

Thank you also to Thierry Bahizi who was present during much of Theo's journey and generously permitted us to share part of his life-story, too.

Thank you Alison Guinness for introducing me to Theo. You believed this story needed to be told and spent hours recording Theo's testimony. Without your unrelenting and generous support, efforts and prayers, *My Country Wept* couldn't have been published. And thank you to Simon Guillebaud who encouraged us to complete the manuscript and get Theo's testimony out.

Thank you to both Theo's family and my own. To Theo's wife Christine, and his children Précise, Prévoyant, Kerry Princia and Danny Prince. To my husband Josh and three daughters Grace, Bella and Hannah. We are grateful for your unwavering love and giving us the time and space in our busy lives to complete this project.

And finally, thank you to my parents, Mary and Puvi, and my sister Judi. I will always be thankful for the way you have championed my writing and for your tremendous love for Christ which has permeated my own life, too.

Further Information

Theo occasionally visits the UK and can be contacted at: mbazetheo@yahoo.com.

Shortly before publication, Rema Ministries changed its name to Rema Burundi, following a new law governing NGOs which would have led to it being classified as a church. For more information about Rema Burundi, please visit remauk.org.

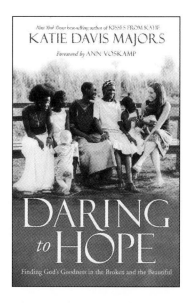

Daring to Hope

Finding God's goodness in the broken and the beautiful

Katie Davis Majors

The sequel to *Kisses from Katie* sees Katie still in Uganda looking after her thirteen adopted girls. But after unexpected tragedy shakes her family, Katie begins to wonder, *Is God really good? Does he really love us?*

Daring to Hope is an invitation to cling to the God of the impossible – the God who whispers his love to us in the quiet, in the mundane, when our prayers are not answered the way we want or the miracle doesn't come. It's about a mother discovering the extraordinary strength it takes to be ordinary. It's about choosing faith no matter the circumstance and about encountering God's goodness in the least expected places.

Though your hopes and dreams may take a different shape, you will find your own questions echoed in *Daring to Hope*. You'll be reminded of the gifts of joy in the midst of sorrow. And you'll hear God's whisper: *Hold on to hope. I will meet you here.*

978-1-78078-460-1